Praise for *Real Estate Titans*

"*Real Estate Titans* gives a fantastic overview of what the best investors and developers in the world have done to get to the top—and how you can too."
—Rodrigo Suarez, Co-Founder & Managing
Partner of HASTA Capital

"Erez takes his readers on a journey through his own career and numerous interviews with several of real estate's most successful entrepreneurs. In the process, he distills seven instrumental lessons that are a must-read for every professional, regardless of the stage of their career."
—Ashesh Parikh, Managing Principal at
Lock Three Properties

"Forget all the infomercials promising you real estate wealth with no work and no money down. Educate yourself with the world's elite real estate players who found different ways of creating multi-million and multi-billion dollar real estate companies from scratch. Many of their secrets are in this book, and Erez has done an incredible job summarizing what really matters most. This book will get you on the fast path to success in real estate investing."
—Austin Netzley, Author, Investor, and
Founder & CEO of 2X

"Erez Cohen has discovered the secrets of real estate titans and shares them in this must-read book for anyone who is serious about becoming rich through investing in real estate."
—Brian Zaratzian, Founding Partner
of Omaha Beach Capital

"Erez has assembled an eclectic mix of real estate industry leaders for an intriguing behind-the-scenes look into decision-making at the highest levels."
—Dr. Sam Chandan, Dean of the Schack
Institute of Real Estate at NYU

"A must-read book if you want to achieve extraordinary success in the real estate game. The proven and tested principles shared by the *Real Estate Titans* in this book are simply not available anywhere else. A mind-expanding and thrilling read."

—Mark Anastasi, Author of the New York Times Bestseller
The Laptop Millionaire

"Our industry is a fascinating one and second only to the brilliance of those who lead it. A unique culmination of perspectives that are intriguing in their own right and combined, a powerful take on what it requires to be a titan of real estate. A top read for anyone looking to climb to the top of the Commercial Real Estate ladder."

—Will Friend, CEO of Bisnow

"It would take years of your time and a lot of your energy to travel the world and chase down these real estate icons for an interview. Read this fascinating manual more than once. Each time, you will uncover new insights."

—Andrew Strenk, Global Retail Expert & CEO of Strategic Planning
Concepts International

"The insights and experiences shared from the *Real Estate Titans* in this book are pure GOLD! If you want to learn from the best of the best and conquer real estate investing; I urge you to read this book."

—Joshua Lybolt, President, Lifstyl Real Estate

"Whether you're a full-time real estate entrepreneur or a part-time investor, Real Estate Titans contains wisdom that will be instrumental to making smart decisions and dreaming big."

—Patrick J. McGinnis, Author of *The 10% Entrepreneur* &
Host of the podcast *FOMO Sapiens*

"Erez—and the titans he interviewed—are authorities on real estate. If you want to learn how to invest in real estate better than anyone else, read this book now."

—Alan Burak, Hedge Fund Manager & CEO
of Never Alone Capital

REAL ESTATE TITANS

7 KEY LESSONS FROM THE WORLD'S TOP REAL ESTATE INVESTORS

EREZ COHEN

WILEY

For general information on our other products and services or for technical support, please contact our Customer Care Department within the United States at (800) 762-2974, outside the United States at (317) 572-3993 or fax (317) 572-4002.

Wiley publishes in a variety of print and electronic formats and by print-on-demand. Some material included with standard print versions of this book may not be included in e-books or in print-on-demand. If this book refers to media such as a CD or DVD that is not included in the version you purchased, you may download this material at http://booksupport.wiley. com. For more information about Wiley products, visit www.wiley.com.

ISBN 9781119550044 (Hardcover)
ISBN 9781119550082 (ePDF)
ISBN 9781119550075 (ePub)

Printed in the United States of America
V10008240_021319

To Shlomo and Edna

Contents

Acknowledgments

There are so many extraordinary people who helped me in this journey, I am deeply grateful for their untiring encouragement and support.

I would like to thank the Real Estate Titans interviewed in this book, I am deeply grateful that they agreed to share their unique wisdom with the world.

This book would not have been possible without the inspiration, intelligence, and support of Dr. Peter Linneman, who has been a guiding presence in my career. I never stop learning from his prodigious insights and feel deeply privileged to call him my friend.

I would also like to thank two other mentors and close friends: Jaime Lara, my business partner, for his teachings and leadership, and Gerardo Ruiz, for his guidance and optimism.

To my brothers, sisters and other family members, thank you for all your support.

To my friends and industry colleagues: Isaac Sutton, Salomon Sutton, Alan Burak and Sandy Ohebshalom, Varun and Pooja

Mammen, Aman and Amrita Kumar, Ivanka Trump and family, the Alcalay family, the Ohebshalom family, Andrew and Annie Strenk, Tony Robbins, Mark Anastasi, Brian Zaratzian, Yoel Amir, Gili Raichstain, Atul Narayan, Nathalie Virem, Jorge Margain, Rodrigo Suarez, Olivia Schmid, Michael Delmar, Douglas Cain, Jerome Foulon, Gerald Marchel, Clifford Payne, David Orowitz, Elias Fasja and family, Jaime Fasja, Jimmy Arakanji, Sandor Valner, Douglas Linneman, Asuka Nakahara, Jeff Thelen, Laura Figueroa, Jonathan Sizemore, Jason Chow, Ariel Tiger, Blanca Rodriguez, Josefina Moises, Gabriel Patrick, Margarita Infanzon, Adi Weinstein, Lyman Daniels, David Daniels, Bruce Kirsch, Austin Netzley, Ricardo Cervantes, Ricardo Zuñiga, Adrian Aguilera, Héctor Sosa, Fernando Delgado, Ursula Guerra, Santiago Collada, Jose Askenazi, Jose Cohen, Dany Izbitzki, Jennifer Skylakos, Vince Chamasrour, Marcos Sando, Simon Coote, Guillermo Rivera, Rodrigo Lopez, Karen Sanvicente, Jorge Laventman, Abraham Garcia, Mauricio Durante, Sebastian Gonzalez, Enrique Mendez, Juliana Roman, Francisco Navarro, Gihan Neme, Alba Medina, Lorenzo Berho, Mauricio Khalifa, Jorge Henriquez, Elizabeth Bell, Aaron Kraig, Lea Ribeiro de Oliveira, Gleides Noronha, Emily Walter, Patty Aguilar, Karren Henderson, Beth Merrick, Angela Sciandra, Annette Vargas, Debbie Larson, Bianca Ledermann, Doris Goldych, Joseph Warmann, Mark Lack, Peter Voogd, Benjamin L. Shinewald, Wesley Whitaker, and Federico Martin del Campo.

Finally, thank you to my real estate classmates at the Wharton School for sharing with me their passion for business and real estate. I honor you all.

Introduction

"I really think we have a good chance to do this deal," said Ivanka Trump with a glamorous smile, slowly tilting her head toward me.

I was surprised. I had begun to wonder what she could possibly see in these rejections that I didn't. I was sweating profusely, in this majestically decorated office on the 25th floor of Trump Tower, feeling somewhat out of my league. Myriad investors had turned us down. How would a deal possibly come together at this point?

I was not optimistic. A small frustration had grown into an overwhelming sense of apathy, and I was ready to throw in the towel. In my mind it was just too tough to make this deal happen. No matter what our proposal was or how much we were willing to add in value, the investment groups we were negotiating with did not want to go ahead.

Faced by her surprising enthusiasm and confidence, I wondered if there was something I had missed. It became obvious that Ivanka had a different mindset. It would be months before the idea dawned on me that she had the mindset of a Real Estate Titan.

Thanks to her many qualities—among them a powerful mindset, an impressive work ethic, clarity, and resourcefulness—she was indeed able to convince several investors, a few weeks later, to proceed with the investment.

It was summer 2010, and I had just been shown up. I witnessed in person the big leagues of the real estate world. This experience fueled my passion for real estate even more. I decided it was time to embark on a quest.

My Quest to Meet the World's Real Estate Titans

Fresh out of college, I joined a large New York investment banking firm. I guess the partners were motivated by my perseverance and diplomacy, something my father, who made his career as an ambassador, had instilled in me from a young age.

Whether through luck or fortune, I was assigned a position with the real estate group. Just a few short days later, a colleague handed me a real estate textbook with a light blue cover: *Real Estate Finance and Investments: Risks and Opportunities* by Dr. Peter Linneman.[1] That book sparked my love affair with real estate that continues to this day. It equipped me with a strong financial real estate base and the technical terms necessary to navigate the demanding moments of institutional real estate investing.

But not until I worked for Ivanka Trump did I truly commit myself to learning from "the greats" in this field. What inspired these Titans to work so hard and reach such extraordinary levels of success? What are the main traits that propel them to such great achievements? How have these individuals succeeded on a much bigger scale than so many of their competitors? I would get the answers by seeking out these great men and women and by doing my utmost to meet with them personally. It took me a decade.

My quest would bring me into contact with real estate Titans such as Richard Ziman, Richard Mack, Ronald Terwilliger, Chaim Katzman, Elie Horn, Joseph Sitt, Urs Ledermann, Donald Trump and children, Carlos Betancourt, Ronnie Chan, Barry Sternlicht, Sam Zell, Steven Roth, Jonathan Grey, Stephen Ross, David Simon, and others.

"Waking up every day and loving what you do has a direct impact on your quality of life and on the bottom line of your business," the Real Estate Titan Urs Lederman once told me. Richard Mack shared this me: "Knowing the downside of any deal is far more important than knowing the upside." Sam Zell taught me that good risk managers "will never fall in love with the assets or companies they own."

Little did I know that over the span of a decade the hundreds of insights gained from these luminaries would lead me to develop more than 12 million square feet of real estate and be involved in real estates deals totaling more than $3.5 billion throughout Mexico, the United States, and Brazil.

On a trip with a real estate mastermind group in Los Angeles—I now run these get-togethers once a year—one of my real estate billionaire friends said: "Hey Erez, I think you should write a book about real estate. Like, you know, to share the tips you've picked up along the way from the best real estate investors in the world. Few people have had these types of experiences …"

"That's not a bad idea," I said, mulling it over.

"I could call it *Real Estate Titans*."

Making Real Estate Wisdom Go Viral

In Greek mythology the Titans were a race of gods. One of the Titans, Prometheus, decided to help the human race by handing them the gift of fire and teaching them to use it. In a similar way, the Titans in this book have decided to share significant real estate wisdom with you.

I have two goals with this book. The first is to impress upon you—through the many stories and lessons shared by these modern-day Titans—that real estate is a *wonderful* and *important* business.

Wonderful because in my opinion there is no more intriguing, exciting, fun, and rewarding field in which to make a career. For example, you can change the way a city, district, neighborhood, or street looks like and operates. You can create beautifully designed spaces in which people live, work, and play. You can work with cities to create jobs and build new infrastructure. You can create an investment vehicle and take it public. You can raise an institutional fund and invest it in different geographies. You can interact and work with all kinds of people from different ethnicities, religions, nationalities, and academic backgrounds. You can see the world. The possibilities are endless.

In real estate, there are unlimited points of entry. It is the ultimate field for entrepreneurs. You don't need substantial capital to start; you just need to be resourceful. You can access financing. You can access friends and family money. You can use other people's money. You can be in this business owning one property or a thousand.

Important because every person on the planet is exposed to real estate every moment of every day: Real estate is a part of our everyday life, and it plays an integral role in our economy. Historically, real estate is also the greatest source of wealth and savings for most families around the world. According to several professors, in the last few centuries more fortunes have been made in this asset class than in any other.

Real estate is also the largest asset class in the world. According to Savills[2] an international real estate brokerage and advisory firm, the value of global real estate as of 2017 is US$228 trillion (see Figure I.1). This exceeds—by almost a third—the total value of all globally traded equities and securitized debt instruments, which points to the important role that real estate plays in any economy around the world. To add additional perspective on this colossal number, the value of global real estate is 2.8 times higher than the world's total annual income (Gross Domestic Product, or GDP).[3]

My second goal is for you to become a savvier real estate player by learning from the best in the world. Years ago, one of my mentors taught me that the best way to achieve success is go find the best in the world, in whatever field it is you want to pursue, and model them. This is what I have attempted to do in this book. There is no need to reinvent the wheel, simply find the best and learn from them as much as you can. Throughout this publication, you will find intriguing stories and lessons of real estate entrepreneurs with impeccable advice about what to do—and not to do—in real estate.

THE VALUE OF THE WORLD

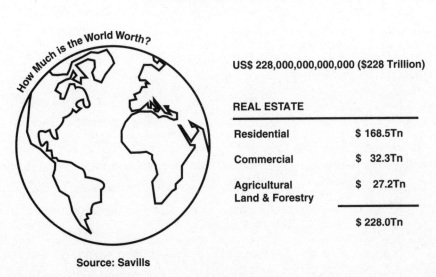

Source: Savills

Figure I.1   The value of the world's real estate.

You will also find 7 key lessons that I extrapolated from these interviews. These lessons include key traits and characteristics I've noticed in each Real Estate Titan I have worked for and interviewed, as well as critical elements of their strategies for success.

If you implement these 7 key lessons in your real estate business—and do the exercises at the end of each lesson—you will see your sales increase and the value of your real estate company take off in a matter of months. The growth will be like nothing you've ever experienced, and once the momentum starts, it will be hard to stop.

Enjoy your journey with the Real Estate Titans!

Notes

1. The latest edition of this textbook also is co-authored by Dr. Peter Linneman and Bruce Kirsch.
2. *Savills World Research Report*, December 2017.
3. *Ibid.*

I

Interviews with Real Estate Titans

The following interviews are intended to share the wisdom of some of the best and most successful real estate investors in the world; however, as you read their compelling stories understand that real estate is driven by logic and experience, and what has worked for one person might not work for another. There is never only one answer or one approach to a real estate deal or a problem. My goal for you is to use their knowledge as a base to embark upon—or continue in—the long and exciting journey of real estate.

These interviews assume that you have the basic knowledge of real estate terms such as yield on cost, internal rate of return (IRR), cap rates, leverage, and more. But if these terms are unfamiliar to you, please refer to the Glossary at the end of the book for definitions and explications.

Chapter 1

Richard Mack

Mack Real Estate Group
New York, New York, USA

Understand the potential downside of a deal

It is a rudimentary principle of portfolio management theory to incorporate alternative assets as part of a diversified portfolio. One of the most popular alternative investments for sophisticated investors is real estate. While it serves as a partial hedge against inflation, it is also a way to enjoy the potential of a steady cash flow stream.

Within the real estate space, institutional investors are probably most attracted to the private equity arena. Real estate private equity funds have been attracting large amounts of capital with assets under management reaching an all-time high as of the end of 2017 of $811 billion.[1] One private equity real estate giant is Richard Mack.

In His Own Words

I was at the top of my class in high school, but not in college. I guess I wanted to have fun, experience being in a fraternity and think creatively away from my major, but I was a hard worker and later regretted my lack of academic discipline in college. By the time I entered college, my father had established himself as a very successful developer. I graduated at a time when people commonly assumed that the son of a successful businessperson was not capable. When I started working, I felt that I had a lot to prove.

I graduated from the Wharton School at the University of Pennsylvania and was very lucky to get a job with Shearson Lehman Hutton. Despite expectations, I didn't always work for my father, and he did not find me my first job. I was fortunate to meet Bill Kahn, a managing director at Shearson Lehman Brothers, in their real estate investment banking group. He took a chance on me. Maybe he saw that I was passionate about hard work and real estate investments. Maybe he wanted a relationship with my father. Either way, he offered me a job, and real estate investment banking seemed a natural fit. I always enjoyed doing things that required self-motivation, creativity, and hard work. I also felt that growing up I had learned a lot about development at the dining room table and that I had an aptitude for real estate. That's pretty much how I ended up getting into the business.

In real estate investment banking in the late 1980s, profit was driven by tax syndications, powered by accelerated depreciation rules for real estate or tax arbitrage. Those loopholes all closed in 1986. By the late 1980s real estate investment banking was in retrenchment. I was forced to restart my career in 1990 just after getting started. Within six months, there was a massive firing across the real estate investment banking division at Shearson. Four of five managing directors and their teams were let go. The one remaining managing director would not even interview me because I was "a rich kid."

Fortunately, I preemptively made two moves: (1) I reached out to my old boss from when I was a summer intern in the facilities department at Shearson, and (2) I applied to law schools. I got the job and shortly after that got into law school.

Shearson was then owned by American Express and their facilities departments were combined. While my experience was brief, I will never forget the lessons that I learned there. The most interesting experience I had in the facilities department, and the one that was the most exciting, occurred during a very weak real estate leasing market. I was sent to Long Island in New York to negotiate with a landlord a renewal for American Express, one of the largest companies in the world. American Express had backup computer systems in a Long Island distribution/office building. The landlord could have tripled the rent and American Express would have stayed: the cost to move the equipment was prohibitive. Instead, I was able to negotiate a significant rent reduction based upon market rents having fallen. This experience made me realize the power of information in real estate, what it means to be a tenant, and what corporations/users see when looking at real estate.

The Big Opportunity

The early 1990s was a really bad time for real estate. As I was graduating from law school, my father invited me to join him in his foray into real estate private equity with Leon Black. They were forming

Apollo Real Estate. With an initial $500 million fund, this untested real estate private equity concept would pursue "distressed" investment opportunities in the United States and Europe. I enjoyed this experience because I got to live through all the initial stages of creating a real estate investment company, the advent of the real estate private equity business, and the highs and lows (but predominantly highs) of successfully closing on many dozens of equity and debt investment opportunities.

So far in my career, I've been involved in the investment of more than $16 billion of equity in real estate transactions all over the globe that I would estimate to have a value of more than $80 billion. While the fund business would prove to be tremendously interesting and lucrative, I always remember the first significant money I made for myself, which was not through the equity fund business. It was something I did on my own, and taught me the value of being opportunistic and the importance of not relying on others (i.e., fund investors) to take a risk that I was not prepared to take on my own.

In my mid-twenties, I bought land with three radio towers on it, paying ground rent, in Montauk, New York. The towers on the land were owned by the tenants, but the land lease was very short. Other buyers at the time were concerned that the tenants would move the towers or that satellites would replace cell towers completely. I was not sure about the technology, but I was pretty sure that the town would not allow these towers to be moved to another location. As a result, I was able to buy the cash flow at a six multiple, a very attractive number to me. I was betting that the underlying demand for users of those towers would increase because cell phone usage would have to increase and that satellite would be too expensive. It was the beginning of the mobile communications era.

I was able to put up the money myself with another partner who wanted to invest. I had to borrow recourse debt, which meant

I had to pledge personal collateral to the bank. Fortunately, after all my diligence and efforts, it turned out that our investment thesis was correct, and demand for these towers skyrocketed.

More importantly, there were no competing radio towers anywhere nearby, and the town was not going to approve new ones. Because of this, I took title to the towers and quadrupled the EBITDA by converting subtenant income into direct income from the telecommunications companies. In retrospect, the investment seems straightforward, but at acquisition this seemed a risky proposition. In fact, I could not get a nonrecourse loan. I had to leverage my whole life in order to get help from the bank. So, I put my guts on the line and I was lucky. Not only was I was able to dramatically increase the NOI, I eventually sold the towers at a 14 multiple.

The lesson to learn from the radio tower deal is that sometimes real estate is mispriced, and for a short period of time, the market players will overlook this. Sometimes, you will see a shift in the market or realize that technology's going to make a change, and you can be one of the people who realize early that the shift will eventually lead to a shift in real estate value. The success of this project left me brimming with confidence and I have tried to leverage these lessons for the benefit of the many partners who have entrusted me with their capital over the years.

The Polish Job

One of my favorite deals took place in Poland in 2004, just before the country joined the European Union. A company called Metro had built a large portfolio of shopping centers all across the nation and was looking to exit. They wanted to take their money out of Poland and start investing in China.

These shopping centers were purpose-built to be occupied by Metro's several large big-box/category killer concepts. Metro had a hypermarket tenant, an electronics retailer tenant, a "do it yourself"/Home Depot tenant, a "dress for less" tenant, and a big-box sports concept. Metro would add a McDonalds, a video store, and other service tenants to the mix and create a big-box center/mall. They built these centers as a way to have a first mover advantage and launch their retailers in Poland quickly. Metro had no reason to own the real estate long term; they had better uses for their capital than real estate and therefore, they just wanted out of the Polish hard assets. They had tried to list the portfolio on the Polish stock exchange as a REIT. When this failed, they valued certainty. This allowed us to negotiate a good deal. We bought these shopping centers for €775 million, refinanced them at €840 million a year later, when Poland formally entered the EU, and then sold 50 percent of the properties at an even higher valuation. We were able to generate an annualized rate of return of more than 100 percent on that deal over a long hold period and a multiple on equity of more than 5x—not because I'm a genius, but because we made the right call on Poland early and had the right partner in the Mitzner family. When Metro needed to sell quickly and wanted an experienced landlord in Poland that they could trust and live with over a long term, we were the natural choice. Apollo-Rida, our joint venture with the Mitzners, was established and ready to take advantage of the opportunity.

How did this happen? In 1996 a famous Pole and former professional tennis player, Woitek Fibak, took me on my first trip to Poland. After that trip I became convinced that Poland was never going back to communism. This was not a universally held belief.

However, I also realized that most of the local real estate people were inexperienced, or, worse, were likely to try to take advantage of a foreign investor. Luckily, we had a relationship with the Mitzner family. The patriarch was a Holocaust survivor who had moved back to Warsaw.

Apollo-Rida built its first office building in Poland with an 18 percent unlevered yield on cost, something unheard of in the West. That was followed by many more developments and acquisitions, including the acquisition of the Warsaw Trade Tower from Daewoo of Korea.

In 1996, I bet that Poland was headed in the direction of the West. I thought that they would be allowed into the European Union, their market would grow rather than shrink, and the value of these properties would rise—but I had to convince my partners, which was not easy. I had to make a compelling case.

During my time there, I saw massive opportunity. There was a large supply-and-demand imbalance. Demand was four to five times higher than supply, according to the market info I gathered. Before you begin to think that I'm clairvoyant, I didn't discover these numbers simply walking around office buildings, warehouse buildings, and shopping centers and watching people; together with the Mitzners we spent significant time with brokers, market consultants, tenants, and customers. The local leasing brokers would provide lists of tenants that could not find space. Incredibly, these tenants were major credit multinationals. Their demand was well in excess of the existing stock of modern space.

At the time, many investors were bearish and worried that Poland would slide back into communism, taking their investments with it. Rather than listen to newspapers or pundits on television, I went to speak in person to the people who were living in this economy. We discussed the growing middle class and the availability of low-cost labor. The information I gathered got me very excited. I concluded that the availability of cheap, well-educated labor and a large population starved for Western products would be irresistible to multinational companies that wished to produce and sell in country.

People kept asking me, "Are they going back to communism?" I was just a kid at the time, but it was people my age who were to determine Poland's future. They wanted freedom and prosperity and I saw they were prepared to work hard to achieve them. It was being on the ground and speaking to a myriad of people that allowed me to make a comfortable bet against Poland's reversion back to communism.

The venture finally sold off its last shares in that deal in 2018, more than 20 years after my first trip. In this deal, like others before and some that would come, I realized that information is a very big advantage. You just can't beat the value of local knowledge and boots on the ground.

Local Knowledge

Often money is made on the macro side of investing; you get the trend right and the trend is your friend. Buying real estate from the Resolution Trust Corporation (RTC) in the early 1990s was one of these great macro bets. Macro bets in real estate tend to be cyclical bets about timing, which means that you need to be able to make micro bets to generate excess returns when markets are in equilibrium. As it relates to micro bets, it is important to realize that land appreciating in value is the primary way to make money in real estate, because buildings depreciate. And that always comes down to location.

Knowing the details of the region where you are investing is of critical importance in real estate. Profit in purchasing land is the combination of local knowledge to find the right property and an understanding the macro principle of where you are in the current real estate cycle.

To succeed as a developer, I deeply believe you must stick to the region you know the best. You must understand the micro. Going outside your local area can be very dangerous—which leads me to my worst deal.

The Radio Tower King

After my success with the radio tower deal in Montauk, I thought to myself, "Hey, I know some things about radio towers. Now that we are doing private equity deals, let's go and do more." While we were looking for a large investment opportunity in radio towers, two junior members of my team uncovered something that seemed interesting. It was the opportunity to buy a radio tower construction firm.

The contractor's pitch was that communication companies were asking him to deploy cell equipment towers and when no tower was built in a coverage area, he would be able to build them and lease space to the carriers. Unfortunately, this sale/leaseback pitch was simply not true.

I was a young 30-something back then, relying on very bright 20-somethings. Bottom line, we did not perform sufficient due diligence on the construction partner because we wanted to believe that he was acting in good faith. Unfortunately for us, he was not. Additionally, the numbers convinced us that it didn't matter if we built towers at all because the income from construction itself was so good.

The problem was that the projections provided to us were wildly optimistic and bordering on fraudulent. Our business was real estate, and getting into contracting, which is a completely different industry, required a different skill set. We discovered that the contractors were lying to us about their ability to land contracts and own the towers. We got played.

We had a really good idea, but a good idea is not enough to guarantee success on its own. If you invest with the wrong people, rely on flawed documentation, or don't fully understand the mechanics of the asset, you are doomed to failure.

I accept full responsibility for the loss we took on this investment. These mistakes led my worst deal to directly follow my first exciting deal. It was a good lesson.

The Stroke of a Pen

A single law change—the 1986 tax reform bill—put more than a few developers out of business. But in retrospect, it was this change in the tax law in the mid-1980s that set up Apollo and other real estate private equity fund managers for success. In the early 1990s, our company, Apollo Real Estate, made a great deal of money cleaning up the excesses that resulted from overdevelopment, overvaluation, and overlending in the 1980s.

Because of accelerated depreciation and tax syndication, many investments were made purely for tax reasons. When the law on accelerated depreciation changed, values collapsed and many real estate developers and banks lost a lot of money. The Resolution Trust Company was created to clean up the mess—to liquidate the assets of the banks and savings and loan companies.

In response to the unprecedented need for real estate capital, many of the large institutions that dominate the real estate market today were created or expanded dramatically. Real estate private equity funds, commercial mortgage-backed securities, and real estate investment trusts are examples.

Investment Philosophy

There are two primary areas you must understand to succeed in real estate: The micro and the macro, or the overall state of the real estate business and the particulars of each deal.

The most important question I ask myself in any deal is, "What is the current or expected cash flow that the property is producing and why?"

Determining this cash flow is critical. Although there are many subjective factors in every single deal, knowing how much money a property can generate is the one objective fact you can base your decisions on. You're looking at both absolute and relative returns. You can assess if the risk and returns warrant the investments.

Talking about numbers and assessing risk isn't nearly as glamorous or exciting as the subjective factors. Everyone thinks they are more important and love to talk about them, but those factors change all the time.

Don't get caught up in that conversation just because it's interesting. Focus on the factors that remain consistent. I always ask myself two questions when assessing an opportunity:

1. What do I firmly believe about this property that other people don't believe?
2. If I'm wrong, what happens to me and to my investors?

The second question is far more important than the first. I'm trying to assess the potential downside. What will happen if every single one of my beliefs and assumptions is completely wrong? How hard will the downside be?

Knowing the downside of any deal is far more important than knowing the upside. When you are using this critical thinking process, success comes down to whoever has the better information.

Within real estate investing at the property level, assets are usually clustered into four main categories based on investment strategy and perceived risk (see Figure 1.1):

THE REAL ESTATE RISK SPECTRUM

	Core	Core-Plus	Value-Add	Opportunistic
Less Risk ← ─────────── **Investment Profile** ─────────── → **More Risk**				
Sample Transaction	Acquisition of a well-occupied, stable cash-flowing office or apartment building in an established sub-market	Acquisition of Core-type property that needs some relatively minor enhancement; sub-market can be secondary.	Significant value enhancement needed through operating, releasing or re-development.	Re-positioning of ailing properties; Ground-up development; Emerging market investments; Buying entire companies with owned operating assets.
Target Levered IRR	7 - 9%	9 - 12%	12 - 16%	16%+
Leverage Employed	0 - 30%	> 30% <= 60%	> 60% <= 70%	> 70%

Source: Real Estate Finance and Investments: Risks and Opportunities Textbook

Figure 1.1 Four categories along the spectrum of real estate risk.

Starting Over

New real estate investors like to ask me what I would do if I were starting over. Most people at the top of the mountain struggle to give actionable advice because they are too far removed. They don't remember what it's like at the start of their journey. It was too long ago.

When seeking a mentor and wisdom, approach local investors and try to find someone who is doing what you want to be doing in real estate—someone who is more successful than you and still remembers what it's like to be in your position.

I started my real estate career almost 30 years ago and, as much as I'd like to say my memory is rock solid, my perspective is inevitably going to be colored by the lens of time.

Big Opportunities

In the United States right now, because of the regulatory environment, I see institutional ownership of debt as a very good opportunity with good risk-adjusted returns. In Europe, I consider value-add to be a more interesting space. In Mexico and Latin America, mezzanine financing and preferred equity for development is an interesting opportunity.

In Asia, in general, it's very tough to get in as an outside investor, particularly in China. It's going to take a period of local financial distress for us private equity outsiders to get a real foothold there. Watch the news for an Asian downturn or a time for Asian businesses to be more open to outside investment, especially in mainland China. That's when the opportunities will start to appear.

Emerging markets in the world offer the biggest growth opportunities, but they also have the biggest risk. Growth is not only an indication of opportunity in real estate; sometimes, the flow of capital can be even more important.

You have to find the right fit to match your passion. If you are looking to get into property development, and you want to be at the start of something brilliant, then you can go to emerging markets. They're building new things and taking amazing risks, and you can really create. You can be there for the first chapter of the story.

If your primary goal is to not lose money, there are better markets in which to focus your attention. A lot of people use real estate to support their pension, not just as a resource, but to provide returns later in life. That means you can take a lower risk for a lower return investment. That's also a good approach.

A Little Leverage

Our business at Mack Real Estate Group has been building a lot of multifamily properties because home ownership has declined significantly in the last ten years. Right now, it's shifting to a renter's market.

As you look at the United States, the two biggest assets are in decline: office space and retail space. Having said that, there will be some great winners and losers in each of these segments, so you need to evaluate every single company on an individual basis.

Real estate financing is like a drug; if you use it correctly, it can have incredible beneficial results. But if you overuse it, then it can kill you.

Real estate is such a capital-intensive business. It's very convenient to leverage debt, but the danger of debt is that a single shift in the market can push you underwater. This happened to so many developers early in the 1990s, and it's how we were able to buy assets at very favorable prices.

In developed economies, it's very hard to make projects work without the prudent use of leverage. Everything's so expensive in developed spaces. You have to be far more strategic in order to achieve significant returns.

The success of every project is determined by timing. Be aware of how the markets are shifting and where the real estate market is in each cycle. We're in the second-longest expansion in the United States´ history right now. Believe it or not, that bubble's going to wear off soon. Valuations have increased dramatically over the last eight years (since 2010), but you should be prepared for that next downturn; it might be a harsh one.

Not every piece of investment wisdom comes from the world of finance. Wayne Gretzky, one of the greatest hockey players of all time, said what made him great is that he skates to where the puck is going to be, not where it currently is. It's the power of anticipating. I apply this to real estate to mean filling the needs that currently don't exist but where you believe the demand is coming, and having the vision to see that clearly. The most important thing when it comes to investing successfully in the real estate market is to see where the market is going to be in one, two, and five years.

The biggest mistake people make is when they believe in their own nonsense and get high on their own supply. It's where you engage in speculative behavior because of overconfidence. Do not believe in yourself 100 percent; always hedge your risk.

If you slip from strategic investment into speculating, if your success depends upon a shift in the market, be prepared to lose. Speculating is where a lot of money is made, but it's also where a lot of money is lost. When people speculate, they ignore the downside, and often, that downside comes calling. True long-term and strategic investing is about limiting your downside and being patient. There is a difference.

With every single deal—and I can't stress this enough—it's better to seek for a smaller downside than a bigger upside. There's always another deal, whether very big or very small. No matter how long one stays in this game, and no matter how successful someone is, everyone has a story about a deal that went bad. Most of the deals that go bad do so because someone got overconfident and ignored the potential downside.

It's exciting to get in real estate. It gets your blood pumping. There's so much opportunity. But it's also where so many people fail. As you look at every deal, as you approach every opportunity, do not get blinded by overconfidence. Never tell yourself that this is the one deal that won't go wrong.

Technology

Technology will have a big impact on real estate, but it will probably affect it less than other industries. Retail is already getting disrupted, and e-commerce does need physical space. That's why distribution is doing so well. Retail is probably going to need smaller spaces that are closer to home.

People continue to build offices, but office densification, office hoteling, outsourcing, and artificial intelligence are not bullish trends for office space.

Technology has led to a shift in the supply side of the hotel business. Every single person renting a room or their home on Airbnb is now in the hotel business. This platform will fundamentally change the hotel industry, but that industry will not go away. Ultimately, certain people will still want to stay in hotels. The extras that hotels offer will become more critical: the hotel restaurant, the concierge, the superior experience, and the help. When you stay at a hotel and ask for directions, they hand you a map. They'll call a taxi for you. We can do most of those things with apps now. But that experience, the ability to have room service and great amenities, is what will keep hotels from shutting down.

People still like hospitality. They like experiences. They like flexibility. They will pay for them. This truth applies not just to the hotel market but to the residential, office, and retail markets. This is one of the lessons we all need to take from the emergence of coworking companies.

Keep the Faith

Mindset and skills are not the same things. You have to strengthen your mindset, or success is not a possibility. If you don't believe in yourself, nobody else will.

This is where the advice gets hard: How do you find a balance between not believing in yourself and believing in yourself too much?

Instead of constantly struggling to find the right balance in how much to trust yourself, make your decisions from a place of logic and not emotion. Study the risk and potential downside of each deal before making any decision. Surround yourself with people who will disagree with you.

This will help you to stay in between those two ends of the market—from going too slow to going too fast, from not believing in yourself enough to try and make any deal to believing in yourself so much that you make a bad deal. In between, we can maintain our balance with proper research, information, and numbers.

It's important to be self-critical and to maintain the balance between humility and confidence. It's a very fine line, and every day, you have to wake up and walk that line without veering too far to either side.

People who lack humility might be right on numerous occasions. But when they are wrong, they rarely get second chances.

As a leader and investor, be humble and allow people around you to speak up and give you the input you need. Pair a belief in yourself with a strong sense of humility.

If we lack technical skills, believing in ourselves can be very dangerous. We need to combine our research, knowledge, and experience with belief, and that's when we can achieve real success.

My Philosophy

I'm very fortunate that my role model and mentor is my father—someone I respect so much both as a human being and as a businessman. He has a great deal of respect for everyone around him. His commitment to giving back to the community has been deeply instilled within me, and he taught me the honor of keeping my word, understanding that the world is round, and that behaving honorably has its own rewards.

I'm a big fan of Theodore Roosevelt. He is the president who transformed the United States into a global leader. He had the vision to do things that might have been expensive and unpopular, like digging the Panama Canal. But he led without fear, and he had the nobility to step away from the presidency. It's an incredible lesson to me on leadership and values.

I read at least one newspaper every single day and several on the weekends. I am a big consumer of nonfiction works, particularly those about leadership and business affairs. I see great value in spending time with my family and exercising. I'm an avid cyclist, and I just love spending time with kids and watching them as they play sports.

This leads me to my final pieces of advice. Your word and your reputation are more important than money. Once you lose those, it doesn't matter how much money you have. People will stop wanting to do deals with you, or they'll look at ways to get just a little bit more out of you.

Being productive is one of the keys to self-worth. No matter how successful you get, it's never time to sit on your laurels. Selflessness is the key to happiness. You get more when you give than when you get. Contributing to society is wrapped up in hard work; work hard so you can give back more. You can't take anything with you when you pass away. All you have left are the good deeds you carried out in this life, and those are the most important things.

Key Principles

- Having access to good information should provide you with power.
- There are times in every cycle where some real estate is mispriced, and for a short period of time, the market players will overlook this. Work diligently to find these opportunities.

- It's very convenient to debt, but the danger of debt is that a few small shifts in the market can cause you to lose your entire investment. If you use debt, do so prudently.

- Land appreciating in value is the primary way you make money in real estate. And that always comes down to location and timing. To be profitable when purchasing real estate, you must have local knowledge to find the right property and to understand where you are in the current real estate cycle, which is timing.

- If you are a real estate developer or plan to be one, you should focus on the region you know best. Going outside your local area can be very dangerous.

- Be humble and surround yourself with smart people who will tell you what they think.

- Keeping your word and behaving honorably has wonderful rewards.

Exercise

When we look to invest in the stock market we are usually inundated with warnings regarding the inherent risks involved in this potential investment. In real estate, however, the average person is more likely to see advertisements claiming just the opposite: that it is easy to make quick money and take no risk. This is almost never the case. Prudent investors understand that if they are in the business of real estate they are in the business of taking risks, and they must become expert risk managers. The key is to learn how to mitigate risk. Therefore, imagine you had a $100 million dollar fund right now to go invest in real estate, where would you be in the risk return spectrum? Are you prone to taking on higher risk to get higher returns and are therefore opportunistic? Which sectors in real estate would you look to invest in? Why? What geographies? How would you mitigate most of the risks?

Notes

1. 2018 *Preqin Global Real Estate Report.*

Chapter 2

Urs Ledermann

Ledermann Holding AG
Zurich, Switzerland

Your final users should be your biggest fans

S uccessful people throughout history have been visionaries who reimagined industries and niches within industries. From his own humble beginnings Urs Ledermann has understood this important concept. Although I learned several things from my long talk with him, perhaps none were as interesting to me as his belief that the best way to predict the future is to create it.

Humble Beginnings

I don't come from a real estate family, and I certainly didn't study real estate at university. I began my career as a headhunter, finding the perfect employees for large corporations seeking the best talent. I saw there was an open niche in the market at the time, and I wanted to solve this problem.

Although I enjoyed building a business in the headhunting game, I was quite aware of the volatility of the market. Companies have roles they want to be filled, and they bring you in to find the perfect employee. When you succeed, you make a nice commission, but a shrinking economy causes the entire headhunting industry to disappear. If companies aren't seeking new employees, my entire customer base disappears.

I was in my early 20s and decided that it would be nice to have a house and find a way to balance out my income. I was seeking a source of revenue that would not be as vulnerable to shifts in the market. If my clients went through a season where demand was low for new employees, I could stay afloat with a steady income stream.

My office was actually inside a beautiful building. Having appreciated the surroundings for some time, I decided I wanted to own the building. I called my landlord, but he did not appreciate my idea. He shouted at me, saying the house was not for sale.

He was very upset, but I was very determined. I called him again a week later, and he finally decided to meet me. He invited me to a traditional private members club for gentlemen; perhaps he thought the environment would freak me out because I was so young. But I wasn't willing to let his plan distract me.

By the end of that night, we had an agreement. I was 23 years old, and I bought that house with a handshake and a $150,000 down payment.

It was a considerable risk for me to buy a house that I did not have the equity to purchase. I needed to accrue $450,000 in the next twelve months or I would lose my deposit. Stabilizing the volatility of my headhunting business was critical, so I was willing to work extra hours and put in extra effort in order to take control of this asset, even though I was placing myself in a substantial amount of jeopardy with my handshake and deposit.

I planned to rent out the rest of the house where I had my office because the building was so large. I learned a valuable lesson with my first deal—real estate is a very slow business, you need to see it as long-term.

In the United States, people buy and sell houses within three months to make a profit, but in Switzerland, this is impossible. The real estate process moves very slowly.

Nobody sells a property within two years of purchase because taxes are brutal. Refurbishments or investments into properties are difficult for many investors in the short-term due to tax restrictions and tight permitting and construction regulations.

Headhunting is a very fast, short-term profit-oriented business; real estate was a massive change of pace for me. It's very tempting to become attached to properties emotionally. During this time, I had to learn how to wait. I had to learn patience.

My growth in this business was meteoric because of my ability to be patient.

Reimagine the Vision

I recall seeing a commercial property, called "Kirchenweg," designed and erected by the world-renowned architects Haefeli, Moser, and Steiger. Unfortunately, the project was too complex and too expensive at the time to obtain. It's a listed building under protection, which is something that I normally appreciate. But Swiss industrialists owned the building, and the president of the company was hoping to get a higher price than we were comfortable offering.

Properties to me have energy; this energy in some way communicates with me. I explained this thought to him, saying that when the house was ready to be sold, Kirchenweg would come to me. He was shocked at the way I attempted to negotiate a sale. Four weeks later, his managing director called me and responded that the house was ready for me.

A building has to fit you and your lifestyle. We purchased the real estate and invested five years reconstructing and repositioning the building, within the protected parameter, to where it is today, with the assistance of a new star architect, Tilla Theus, who brought it back to life in a new light while preserving the old soul. I knew that employees would also want a fun experience while at work. Switzerland permits were very slow, and it took a much longer time than expected. But we waited and we were patient. Again, patience paid off, and we developed exactly what we were looking for. Such journeys, though grueling, become pillars in your career – and gems in your portfolio.

Seeking Beauty

Our company works vigorously to create and retain exceptional quality structures that stand out at first sight. It doesn't feel like you're entering just another building. They encompass a unique identity that differentiates them from the masses.

How many times have you driven into the parking garage of a building and suddenly wondered where you were because every garage is similar and mundane? This to me was a problem that needed correcting. I wanted to have exclusive and inviting garages in my properties to offer an experience as welcoming as you'd expect upon entering your living room.

The true dedication lies in making our apartments as well as our commercial and retail spaces enjoyable in the long run; for example, we commission artists to create pieces tailored to each building. More often than not I encourage artists to bring me ideas associated with the building. At the deepest level, this can make a huge difference. It allows you to create something that's one of a kind, with an artistic brilliance to it that I would never be able to come up with on my own. We want our residents to love where they live, so there needs to be something special about their environment, whether they're living or working there.

I also want our residents to be proud of where they live. Although this may seem like hyperbole to many, I believe that if you live in a nice building in pleasing surroundings, it encourages you to behave accordingly in your daily interactions. I am willing to reduce my short-term profits in exchange for long-term rewards. When you get people in a pleasant environment like that, they're proud to be there and tend to stay, which results in lower turnover. Additionally, our units are treated with greater respect and attention, which in turn decreases overall reoccurring repair and capital improvement expenditures.

Doing things differently than other developers, and extending our services beyond standard industry practice, has allowed me the opportunity to reach my true aspirations. Our buildings offer a concierge service to cater to all our client's needs. Having this regular and intimate interaction fosters with them fosters a healthy relationship and provides an extraordinary experience. Every time I'm working on a building or property, I ask myself this very simple question: "Would I let my daughters live here? Would they be happy living here? Would I live here?"

Not All Roses

Refinancing negotiations can make already intricate real estate projects more complicated. I believe that you simply can't trust bankers. They're not partners, and they have a complete inability to think long-term. Because they're short sighted, always looking for the quickest buck, you have to be very careful with bankers.

Real estate goes through cycles, as economies expand and recede. During a recession, people often have the following thought: "The economy is shrinking. I have to lower my prices because something has happened to the system."

But you must be able to think differently and say to yourself, "What are the options if I can't sell this property? Maybe I can rent it out instead of selling it." Maybe you can buy the adjacent properties and create something new. When a crisis arises, it comes unexpected, so you need a plan and an exit strategy in place for any unforeseen uncertainty.

I have a very clear focus: I only invest in urban areas. Most importantly I mostly invest in what the real estate industry considers "irreplaceable" locations, the timeless properties that will appreciate in value and preserve their quality over the long run. This has a positive effect on the overall appraisal of the portfolio. In these types of urban environments, you can't do a lot of demolition and new construction development. There are so many barriers to cross that the typical property owner has a difficult time successfully entering the market. The risks are too high. It's much smarter to renovate or plan minor alterations to an existing structure that does not require total demolition. What you want are the irreplaceable locations.

Miami overbuilds residential buildings because developers might believe that everybody wants to live there, but it's all based on speculation. They target overseas markets – Russian, Brazilian, and others—because they successfully convince them that Miami is a secure place to invest. But these buildings are empty most of the year.

I know a luxury building in Miami that is top of the line, and only four families live in the entire complex. It's a ghost building. That is not my philosophy. I don't think of buildings as profit centers. I think of them as wonderful places for people. A building has energy and life. Without people living in a building, it's nothing. This philosophy that sees the residents as an integral part of any building has been critical to my success in real estate. When I'm analyzing a real estate property, there are certain things that I look for.

For instance, I lived in Boston for three and a half years when my children were young. At the time I couldn't speak English, so I decided to hire a university professor to develop my base in the language and further my IT skills. My time there taught me a little bit about the area.

So after selling my recruitment business, I thought, "I'm rich now. I never have to work again." I began to remember how much I enjoyed my time in Boston and how vibrant the city is.

There are so many young people and universities; pharma and health play a huge role, the financial sector is rapidly growing, as are lots of other important businesses. What's beautiful about this old city is that you don't have to worry about new construction because everything in the city is built, which I absolutely love. There's a little new construction planned for in the harbor area, but there's no competition for what the city already offers.

My initial idea was to open up some new revenue streams outside of Europe, and I thought it would be nice to have some exposure in the United States. Doing business in a new region is all about meeting the right people, and I was lucky enough to meet the right ones to fit my needs.

In Europe, business relationships are more relaxed. I coach people, and people coach me. It's not just business; it's also a friendship. It's easier to trust each other in Europe than it is in the

United States. Unfortunately, my experience with Americans has often been about the dollar. Everything is cash. Nobody takes anybody's word, and everybody's impatient and paranoid. Remember: I closed my very first deal by paying $150,000 on a handshake. I never once had to wonder if my landlord would honor that deal, and I never once had to worry whether we signed a contract.

In the United States, you can't do business with a handshake anymore. In Europe, once we sign a deal, it takes some time to complete the acquisition transaction. We can wait thirty or sixty days because we trust that a foundation has been established. It has to be fun to go to the office. We don't want the stress of calling someone every day and asking, "Where's that money?"

Because we do our due diligence and know who we're dealing with, we know that the funds will reach us in a timely fashion, so we're not worried that we're going to give away a property and never receive the money. That's never a fear.

Starting Over

If I were starting off in real estate today, I would be more invested in the big cities in the United States. New York City is going to be there forever. It has long-term appreciation. Assuming you bought a piece of land at market price, property in Manhattan will always go up in value in the long-term.

I'm also interested in looking at opportunities in Asia, especially China and India. I live in Europe – it's where I'm from, and it's a great continent. It will always attract tourists, but I like the residential sector. I like co-living areas. I think that's so fascinating, and it's where my heart and my passions lie.

Passion is the most important thing in real estate. We like to dream a lot, and we're constantly coming up with new experiences for living. You must be a little bit crazy when you're comparing yourself to the average person so that you can dream up and build amazing buildings that people desire to live in and see themselves living in for a very long time. You need to be a visionary and fix a problem for people. Sometimes people don't know what they want, and you have to show it to them. Create a new experience for your users; make sure they have fun.

Real estate is a long-term business. Buying, fixing, and selling properties can take years. You will likely ride an entire real estate cycle in your career. Be prepared for the ups and the downs and avoid speculation.

Focus on developing strategies that are recession-proof and that will allow you to survive a downturn in the market, a change in the demographics, or unexpected geopolitical events. Write down your goals and your dreams. Review them every night before going to sleep. This will ensure that you achieve them.

You need to have very clear goals. The biggest mistake real estate players make is getting emotionally attached to their investments. That's dangerous. In this business, you have to push your emotions aside. There's no space for emotion when you're managing other investors' money because you have to be a fiduciary, and you have to serve your shareholders. You must be fiscally disciplined to succeed and grow in real estate.

When you're using other people's money, you have to treat it with more respect than you'd even treat your own. Don't allow your emotion to cause you to spend someone else's money on the wrong deal. The other mistake is not having local knowledge. I used to be on the board of a company owned by a Russian oligarch and a Swiss real estate firm. They were buying houses all over Germany, Holland, Switzerland, and some other countries with no idea about the local markets. This left them vulnerable, and they took a massive hit.

Like everything else, even at the highest levels, there are good and bad players. Someone small can outmaneuver a massive international company with billions of dollars when they understand their local market in a deep and meaningful way.

Learning by Doing

Unfortunately, I don't think you can learn everything about real estate investing by simply attaining a degree at a university. A lot of it comes from going out there and doing it. As much as this book is filled with the knowledge and experiences of successful real estate investors from around the world, their wisdom will never become yours unless you take that knowledge and experiment as you execute your deals.

I'm a big believer in learning out in the world, the way that I did. I believe that questioning everything is part of this process. When you invest your own money, that learning curve is going to be steep. But when you work for other people, and you lose their money, you're not going to learn as much because it's not your money. It doesn't mean as much to you.

My grandfather was a farmer, and he told me when I was a child that I had to be an owner, not an employee. When you work for a company, you have many external risks. But when you're the owner, you only have yourself to blame.

I was fortunate to have great teachers at school. I learned a great deal about real estate from friends and real estate entrepreneurs, but I'm still learning. You have to maintain your curiosity. Sometimes, I call other great investors and developers and meet with them just to listen to them and learn. I want to hear their philosophies and how they see the world.

I love to read newspapers every single morning because it keeps me informed about the world, and what I see in these articles allows me to communicate with other people. I also love reading biographies. Reading the stories of the greatest figures in human history allows you to discern their similarities and figure out what made them so great.

I own private estates around the world in Europe and in the United States, but when I'm home, I'm always up early and start the day with a light 20-minute exercise and stretching routine. Sometimes, I like to go to the beach and relax as a way to step out of my business. That's when I often come up with my best ideas. I am dedicated to taking long walks to think, and I play golf to keep myself moving, which also allows for me to be in the flow of the moment. Something that I really do and not just preach is live in the moment. I fully embrace situations and experiences, whether in the workplace or in private. I truly live by the philosophy of being mindful and aware. Also being in the moment with those you interact with is a very important trait I foster. I take the time and I am in the moment with that individual.

No matter what you do, have fun and enjoy the journey. Enjoy every single day. It doesn't matter if you have 100 or 200 buildings when you're lying in that casket. When my time comes I sure hope that I can say, "That was fun! I enjoyed my time on earth."

I encourage you to live a happy life. If you don't like your life, go and change it; start something new that you love. If you hate real estate, you hate the thought of negotiating, or you hate everything about this business other than the fact that you make a lot of money, don't do it. There are loads of other things you can do to make money that you will actually enjoy. You could take the principles of this book and apply them to other industries and still find great value from these lessons.

You have the ability to make your own destiny. I encourage you to try and be a good person. Don't be greedy and don't step on others on the way to the top.

I hope that some of my stories have encouraged you. I believe that real estate can be a beautiful thing; you can really build and design beautiful homes and places for people to live, even if you're doing it one family home at a time.

Key Principles

- Challenges will always arise when you try to pursue opportunities in real estate; never allow them to stop you from accomplishing your goal.

- The best entrepreneurs in real estate are usually innovators because they have to use their money wisely.

- Do everything you can to own a high-quality portfolio of properties that is special and unique.

- It's important to never become complacent or do the same things repeatedly. Focus on adding massive value to your stakeholders, communities, and final users.

- If most or all your real estate peers or competitors are going one way, take it as a sure sign you need to go the other way and do something different and unique.

- Competition based only on price doesn't work. You must compete on knowledge of your industry and your customer, on continuous innovation, and more.

- If you manage other people's money you must be a fiduciary and serve your shareholders.

- Do not only focus on short-term profits; focus on adding massive value to your clients and final users. For the long-term, this will provide the biggest financial rewards.

Exercise

Create your Declaration of Principles as a statement of what you and your real estate business stand for. For example, your brokerage business could model a declaration based on the following three principles: (1) we honor our agreements, whether they are formed in writing or in handshakes; (2) as real estate agents, we take special pride in the assurance that we only present clients with the very best properties in Dallas, Texas; and (3) we hold ourselves to the highest standards of integrity and excellence. When you are true to your principles, it doesn't matter what kinds of challenges present themselves, your principles are a set of powerful tools that will guide your decision-making and serve you along your journey.

Chapter 3

Ronald Terwilliger

Trammell Crow Residential
Dallas, Texas, USA

The secret to living is giving

Of all the Real Estate Titans I had the pleasure of interviewing, none displayed so much passion for addressing
the affordable housing problems in the United States as
Ronald Terwilliger. One of his current life missions, which can be
summed through this quote—"In my philanthropic life, I've tried to
demonstrate my belief that hope begins with access to a decent, affordable home. I want to help ensure a leveraged, sustained impact beyond

my lifetime and inspire others to make the commitment to support affordable housing"—is truly inspiring to hundreds of thousands of people all over the world. Ronald Terwilliger continues to make colossal improvements in the lives of tens of thousands of low-income families around the world by enhancing their housing conditions.

Love What You Do

I have learned that it is important to find an occupation that you truly enjoy. Going to work on Monday morning should be something you look forward to just as much as taking family time on a weekend. My 30 years at Trammell Crow Residential were a great joy to me as I worked in a partnership culture where everyone had aligned interests. We had a work hard/play hard culture, and while the partners became great friends, it was clear that business was our first priority.

I came from a modest beginning growing up in the public school systems of Arlington, Virginia. I was only able to attend the Naval Academy because I was a recruited athlete. At the academy, we had courses that focused on a naval career and I graduated with a degree in Marine Engineering. I served during the Vietnam War and then gradually became disenchanted with a naval career, so I left after five years to attend Harvard Business School. I have always had an intuitive feel for numbers, and after taking one course at Harvard on real estate I decided on real estate development as a career. By joining the Real Estate Club in business school, I was able to meet with real estate companies wanting graduates. I landed at Hilton Head Island in South Carolina working for the Sea Pines Company in recreational community development.

After working at Sea Pines and going through a bankruptcy in 1974, I moved to Dallas, Texas, and became chief financial officer of a commercial construction company. I was restless in that role, and longed to get back to development. My big break occurred when I was offered a partnership by Trammel Crow to move to Atlanta and rebuild Trammell Crow Residential Companies in the eastern United States. Because the recession in 1974–75 decimated Trammell's interests in the east I had to take a pay cut to join the Crow organization, but I was given an ownership of interest in my new company and a chance to build wealth through real estate development.

My second big break was discovering the rental apartment business. I started my first apartment development in an office park in the Cumberland area of Atlanta in 1980. I built that project for $30,000 per unit and sold it a year after completion for $50,000 per unit. I instantly fell in love with the apartment development business.

The Importance of Mentoring

I had two mentors early in my career and greatly appreciated them both. At Hilton Head, Charles Frasier founded the Sea Pines Company and was a visionary developer of environmentally sensitive communities. Charles had studied recreational developments on the East Coast and had an opportunity to develop a new type of community on the south end of Hilton Head Island, South Carolina. Charles was one of the early pioneers with architectural review programs to ensure that all housing as well as commercial structures were compatible with the environment. He not only built golf courses and tennis courts, but he built walking trails and golf cart paths for residents to get through the community without using automobiles. Sea Pines communities were very appealing to vacationers and retirees alike. Unfortunately, Charles had one blind spot, which was risk management. He built our communities using debt from the mortgage REITs from the early 1970s. He borrowed 100 percent of cost at a rate of 5 over prime. In 1974 when the prime rate went to 12.5 percent, he defaulted on all of those loans.

After a three-year stint in the construction industry, I rejoined the development community in Atlanta, where Trammell Crow (the man and the company) took me on as partner. Trammell, who founded the firm, had returned to Dallas after serving in the navy during World War II and began building warehouses. He understood he would need to add to the built environment to satisfy a growing population of returning GIs who were marrying and starting their own families. Trammell created a national development company using a partnership concept. He would use his reputation and financial statement to start new development companies across the United States and soon became the largest developer of commercial and residential real estate in the country. Trammell was an optimistic, charismatic visionary and was unusually generous. His partnership approach enabled many young partners to build wealth, as all partners shared the profits of development. However, similar to Charles Frasier, Trammell thought very little about the downside risk and his company was deeply hurt by the 1974–75 recession and completely floored by the 1989–93 recession.

While I learned the danger of overleveraging the hard way in both companies, I am forever grateful to Charles and Trammell for the opportunities they provided. Because of my experience in the mid-1970 downturn, I limited the leverage Trammell Crow Residential used and am convinced that allowed us to survive the 1989–93 recession. My experience is that we live in a cyclical economy and are unlikely to anticipate the next downturn. Consequently, real estate developers should operate their business on the assumption that there is a recession coming and they will need to survive for at least three years without capital to start any new projects.

Be Realistic

The real estate development business is a risky business. The demand side is certain to be compromised by an economic downturn. Some property types are more vulnerable than others. I find the apartment development business to have one of the best risk/reward relationships because a well-managed apartment will stay full during a downturn, although you will have to adjust rents downward to stay full in a weaker market. The key to responsible financing of apartment developments is to keep construction debt to 75 percent of cost or less and to have construction loan maturities that are long enough to get you through a recession.

Not every new development will be a winner, but you have to understand the downside of each investment. The biggest mistake I made in the rental apartment business was closing on land before we were able to begin construction. As the market heats up late in the cycle, land sellers demand both higher prices and more difficult terms. In the mid-2000s I compromised my risk management principals by agreeing to purchase land with a financial partner well in advance of having building plans complete enough to start construction. The Great Recession came upon us unexpectedly and the banks called the land loans at maturity. Our company guaranteed land loans and our "partners" walked away from their equity investment leaving us to deal with bank loans on apartment land that had fallen in value by more than 50 percent.

Personal guarantees (recourse debt) are something that you should agree to only if you have virtually nothing to lose. In other words, you should never agree to obtain recourse debt. We have used guarantee corporations and subsequently business asset guarantees to satisfy lenders and investors. My current development company capitalized our platform adequately to satisfy our creditors and we have managed to keep enough liquidity to use when necessary. Developers who survive business cycles in real estate have become good risk managers. You must guarantee completion in virtually all instances, but risk sharing beyond that is important. Essentially, you need to be thoughtful about what you guarantee as well as what credit you put at risk with your guarantee.

Real Estate and Recessions

I have already talked about the cyclicality of our economy and the difficulty in anticipating the beginning, duration, and depth of a recession. If you are dependent on development and construction fees during the recession, you will quickly find out that your fees run out before the recession ends – at least in the merchant building apartment development business. You should try to build into your business recurring fees, such as property or asset management fees that continue in periods of limited development activity, so that you have a chance to sustain the organization. Some of my competitors have been forward thinking enough to get into the acquisition business and the fund management business to provide them with fee income throughout the entire business cycle.

During the Great Recession, developers who were unable to make good on their guarantees had an impact on many banks and investors. It seems to me that every recession creates a change in the standard methodology of development financing. Believe it or not, before the 1989–93 recession, developers in the United States were not required to co-invest in their projects; the entire project could be financed by a lender. Peter Linneman writes, "the equitization of real estate" took place in the early 1990s and the modern REIT era began by replacing lots of debt with public equity (see Figure 3.1). Beginning in 1994, Trammell Crow Residential had to begin co-investing in new real

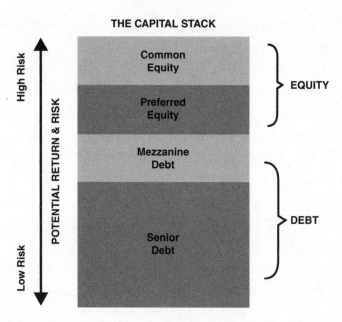

THE CAPITAL STACK

Figure 3.1 The capital stack of real estate, showing low to high risk.

estate developments. Looking back, it is amazing to me that we were not required to have "skin in the game" before then.

After the Great Recession, the banking industry became much more conservative. Construction loans, which are readily available for apartment developments at 80 or even 85 percent of cost, are now hard to obtain at more than 65 percent of cost. New developments are therefore much more conservatively financed and require more capital from developers since the co-invest percentage of the equity required are for construction loans for 50 to 65 percent of cost.

Since I have been in the development business longer than most, I am frequently asked, "What inning are we in?" I don't like the baseball analogy, as I believe no one knows when the next recession will occur or what will cause it. This has been a long expansion, and we have enjoyed lower interest rates and positive leverage on development yields beyond what I have ever experienced.

Rental housing has become necessary for more American families as single-family construction has lagged and construction cost increases have caused fewer families to be able to get a mortgage if they should desire to purchase a home. Demographics in the United States indicate that almost 9 out of 10 new households will be minorities. That fact suggests that rental housing will play an even more important part for housing America's families than it has since the Great Depression.

Keep Learning

Having been in the real estate business for almost 50 years, I realize you must keep learning and adapting. While housing is a fundamental human need, the kind of housing families desire and can afford vary over time. Lifelong learning is a prerequisite to survival in the business.

While real estate is inherently a local business, it is important to stay abreast of national and regional as well as local trends. Many new ideas seem to emanate from California, and right now the risk of rent control is a risk many people are watching carefully.

I am a big fan of the Urban Land Institute and its local District Councils. Participation in an industry association can be educational and broadening. I encourage everyone to keep abreast of new developments and trends.

It is amazing to me that the development side of our industry has been impacted so little by the technological revolution that is taken place. We essentially build buildings the same way we did 30 years ago, and some argue the labor is even less productive because of increased regulation. Incomes are failing to keep pace with project cost increases, and our industry is likely to be forced into product innovation including smaller homes with more density. It's clear to me that American families increasingly want the option to leave their cars at home once they get back from a day's work.

Accordingly, "walk scores" are an increasingly important benchmark to help evaluate the desirability of new locations.

The twenty-first century is likely to result in a lot of changes in technology and alter the nature of jobs and living patterns. We have a housing affordability crisis in this country that will need to be dealt with by government at all levels.

The Two Markets

The United States has two types of real estate markets. The first is supply-constrained markets, and the second is commodity markets.

Examples of supply-constrained markets are those in California and New York. There is the potential to make a great deal of money in these markets since infrastructure is already built. The entry price is very expensive and barriers to entry are high, however, keeping the supply of new housing low.

I am often asked if there is a "first mover advantage" in multi-family real estate. Multifamily rental is typically a commodity business, so this advantage rarely exists. There always has been, and there always will be, plenty of places for families to choose where to live. In addition, there will always be a demand for multifamily real estate.

The key to success in real estate is to have a product that meets the market demands, including the right finishes, the right location, the right mix of units, and the right manager. A truly great property will stay leased through a downturn.

I built my first apartment complex without a mentor to guide me and show me how to succeed in that business. The skills necessary for success in the world of real estate are not the ones most people expect to find when picking up a book like this. You need raw intelligence, vision, culture, and a passion for hard work.

Some of the best developers I have ever seen are the best copiers. They study successful businesses and projects and just replicate them. They don't think they need to create the perfect apartment complex. Instead, they look at what's working.

This is the ideal strategy for new and old investors alike. There is no need to reinvent the wheel or develop a brand-new type of apartment building. A big element of success comes from focusing on what is already working. Building cost-effectively is the key for those in the business of development.

That's the beauty of the Crow organization. The way you can align incentives correctly with charismatic and generous founders, as well as provide a great deal of mentorship within an organization, is magical.

My Philosophy

A few personal philosophies and beliefs have helped me have a successful career. I believe that you should enjoy every single day. Take care of your health and cherish your family. No matter how much money you make, at the end of the day your family is your foundation.

I came from a family of modest means, and I never knew anyone growing up who had money. I grew up in Arlington, Virginia, in a 900-square-foot house. My dad always worked two jobs, and there was not a single year in his life that he earned more than $10,000. His day job was selling wholesale petroleum products. After working his day job, he would come home, take a nap, and then go off to his night job. For a while, he was the late-night manager at a movie theater. Then he became a deputy sheriff.

I inherited my dad's work ethic. I worked all summer, every summer, starting at age 12. I had a different job every year. Delivering newspapers on my bicycle. Inventorying furniture for a moving company. Sweeping the floor at a car dealership, then polishing the used cars. Laying down sod for a landscape company. The extent of the training I received for that position was three words: "green side up."

In my 50s, I began accumulating wealth. I decided to become philanthropic and work with nonprofits as well as becoming a donor for causes I care about. When I die, my family will be taken care of, but the bulk of my estate will be dedicated to developing affordable, decent housing for low-income and disadvantaged people.

Most of my efforts now and my passion for giving are directed toward the affordable housing crisis in the United States (and around the world). I also work hard to help low-income children get an education. I am a beneficiary of the American Dream, and I believe it is important that every American family have an opportunity to improve their lives and avoid multigenerational poverty.

Key Principles

- When investing in any project, focus on the downside before looking at the upside. Ask yourself, "What happens if this deal goes bad?"

- Never borrow money for more than 75 percent of the cost of developing an apartment project.

- If you start developing and a recession hits, you need to remember that recessions typically last for around three years. No one knows when a recession will occur, but everyone should know that it will eventually come and they need to be prepared to survive the period of limited to no new development.

- Do not sign personal guarantees to ensure when things go bad you are not forced into bankruptcy.

- Technology is changing the way we live and work, and it may eventually alter the way we build.

- Demographics are dramatically changing the composition of families and family income in the United States. Unless policy is altered, we are likely to have more low-income renters getting subsidies.

- The secret to life is giving back. Those of us who have benefitted from being born in a capitalistic society could measure our success in life by our family and by how much we have helped others.

Exercise

To be successful in real estate it is very important to learn how financing works. Real estate players typically use financing for four reasons:

1. When they have very little equity to buy the asset and need additional capital.
2. To diversify their portfolios and have a larger number of investments.
3. To improve financial returns. If an investor can obtain debt at a lower interest rate than the yield on cost of an investment, the levered returns should be higher than if that investment was made all equity. A similar concept applies with residential for sale.
4. To obtain the tax shield that comes from servicing the loan (making interest payments). Note that this does not apply in every country, but certainly in advanced economies.

While debt is alluring to any investor, understand that it comes with numerous risks. Investors who have less experience—or are in a desperate situation to secure financing because they feel they might lose a certain deal—may take on debt that charges a higher interest rate than the yield on cost. In this scenario, they will experience negative cash flow, because the net income of the real estate investment is not sufficient to cover the monthly debt service. The investor now needs to find another means of paying for this deficit to avoid a default. Therefore, to avoid this, investors should run different financial scenarios on a spreadsheet to feel confident that their property or investment will generate income to cover the debt service. Investors should have a deep understanding of the projected revenue stream as well as the costs and expenses that will be included in the operations of the property.

If you are looking to borrow money, surround yourself with a trustworthy expert on real estate financing and explain to this person your reasons for wanting to borrow. By understanding why you want to use debt you can better customize your financing needs.

Chapter 4

Gina Diez Barroso

Grupo Diarq
Mexico City, Mexico

A beauty of a mission

In 2004, Gina Diez Barroso founded CENTRO, a university in Mexico City that focuses on the arts. This campus for 2,500 students is the culmination of Barroso's vision for combining design and education in the heart of Mexico City, where the very buildings engage the student's artistic sensibilities.

The campus itself is a garden, with a full third of the available land dedicated to beautiful landscapes and rooftop planting. This university is a physical manifestation of Barroso's belief that art, business, and technology are essential pillars of success, both on and off the campus.

CENTRO is one of the first campuses in the world to meet the stringent environmental requirements to achieve LEED Platinum status. The primary buildings all intersect in the same way the primary disciplines taught at the university intersect. The buildings match the university's philosophy.

The entire campus is a veritable feast for the eyes, including numerous works designed by prominent artists. Unlike many university campuses that are designed separately from the curriculum planning, CENTRO's architecture is integral to every experience on campus.

Starting Out

I began my career at the age of 19, working in the editorial business. Seven years later, I decided to pursue my passion for real estate. I was frustrated by how difficult it was for investors such as myself to launch a real estate project in Mexico due to all the moving parts; developing land was far too complicated and involved.

An investor needed to hire a real estate company that would find and acquire the land for them. They also needed an architect and a construction company, and eventually, a designer to do the interior design. I therefore decided to create a vertically integrated company that could do all these things in-house; I called it Diarq.

I hired people from diverse specialties and ended up having a real estate division with architects on site. I also hired designers for my own construction company. At that time, many foreign investors wanted to do business in Mexico, but they were put off by the logistical complications of building in the country. With so many companies involved, it was hard to get problems solved. When a problem arose, each company could blame the other, leaving frustrated investors wanting to tear their hair out.

By providing a single point of contact with Diarq, investors felt more secure building in Mexico. We began with residential projects, but over time we started to add commercial projects to our portfolio.

Throughout my career I have developed and invested in over 650 projects in Mexico and around the world. I wish that I could say every single one was a success, but some weren't as good as others.

Of all my projects, none is closer to my heart than CENTRO University. It was the first time that I went into education, which became my reason – my purpose and my "why." I finally found my core motivation.

Beside that, it was the first time I built to LEED standards. At first, our goal was to qualify for the Basic LEED, but when we reached that goal, we decided to go for bronze. Then we couldn't resist and went up the ladder of silver, gold, and finally platinum.

We built every inch of the CENTRO campus, both inside and out. We became the only LEED Platinum campus in the world, which was pretty amazing. This project is still my favorite because it combines my passions for design, architecture, education, and the environment.

The Right Project

When looking at an opportunity, I begin by understanding the location, the surrounding market and basic supply and demand dynamics, cost basis, and potential cash flow. The surroundings are very important because I don't usually look to build just a single freestanding building, no matter where in the world I am looking to do the deal. I like to buy the surrounding properties and endeavor to assemble sites. But many times you must deal with problematic owners, tenants, and neighbors. When pursuing this strategy, one of the biggest insights I gained is that costs and timing need to become critical parts of the decision tree. For example, I was involved in one land assemblage where I put together six different properties. The final property, on a per-square-meter basis, was three times more expensive than the average of the whole assemblage. However, I always see real estate as a long-term business (focusing on the equity multiple and not on the IRR, or internal rate of return). So I knew that with time it would become a very good investment.

If I were starting over, I would focus on the residential market or possibly spaces for e-commerce businesses. E-commerce is such a fast-growing sector, especially in urban areas. I'm a little hesitant to get into the office space. In general, the office and industrial sectors are much more similar to the commodity business. What do I mean by this? Historically, many investors have linked the real estate market with the bond market; however, the reality is that some sectors of the real estate market have much higher net operating income (NOI) appreciations than others, so it does not function exactly like a bond. In office and industrial, it used to be the case that you would sign long-term leases (15 to 20 years) and so that type of real estate is very similar to bonds. If you have a company like Estee Lauder leasing 70 percent of your office building or logistical center and paying a base rent with annual inflation, then it's very similar to a bond. However, if you are in the residential for sale segment it could be that prices go up 15 or 20 percent per year because of pent up demand. That is what has happened in Mexico City between 2013 and 2017.

Education is my favorite segment, not because of its financial rewards but its emotional rewards. It's my passion; it fulfills me in a special way.

The Real Estate Business

Real estate is a different animal than many other businesses, and you must be prepared for many challenges. The way you approach real estate is critical. Are you a professional or an investor? These are two drastically different mindsets.

A professional understands the unique nature of real estate and treats it appropriately, but an investor looking to expand a portfolio with a new asset class often doesn't understand the cyclical nature of real estate and the potential downside.

If you want to invest in real estate as an asset class, you have to find properties that will generate income, and you need the financial buffer to endure crises without threatening your other investments. With real estate, you can be affected by economic crises in different parts of the world.

Unfortunately, many real estate investors do not understand the market they are entering, and they often overleverage. (Despite this risk, I think that all investors should have some real estate in their portfolio; it is a great asset class. You have to love bricks and buildings. You must understand that real estate does not operate like other investments.)

Dilettantes entering the real estate market without performing proper research and due diligence make risky decisions and overleverage. Bad timing or downturns, which eventually come, can crush you when you are overleveraged.

As a new investor, work with professionals and keep your debt levels to a minimum. Make sure you are in a strong enough financial position to endure the inevitable market shocks.

Technology

Technology is changing real estate at a surprising pace. I recently read about a center in Germany that is 100 percent automated. It doesn't even have lighting; robots can work in the dark. The world is changing, and everybody needs to adapt. For instance, technology may provide amazing opportunities as cars, gas stations, and towns become more automated, but small gas stations will disappear and small towns may be at a disadvantage (compared to urban areas) as more consumers switch to electric cars.

I have spent time looking at mobility, walkability, how this will evolve and affect real estate. We're now designing to accommodate driverless cars because technology is changing so much. We have not reduced parking in our development projects in Diarq, but at some point, we will. I think the driverless car will bring about a major shift in how the whole world is run and will absolutely have implications on real estate. It could be the case that the driverless car could have an impact on the famous adage of "location, location, location."

Technology is also changing the way we teach at CENTRO. We are shifting to a sharing economy where people find ways to cooperate instead of competing. Those who stick their heads in the sand and ignore how quickly technology is changing the world around them will go the way of the dinosaurs.

To keep high-quality Millennials in your company, providing fun co-working spaces and an inspirational mission might be more important than offering high salaries. Millennials care more about quality of life and changing the world than they do about higher salaries. They are happy to live in smaller, private spaces as long as these include access to better-shared resources and community spaces. This new generation loves to collaborate and share spaces where they eat and work, while the space where they sleep is quite small. When I was young, music was about ownership and possession. You once owned the CD, but now music is shared via apps and digital services.

Millennials are shifting away from possession and toward using more shared resources. Why buy a car when you can rent a bike for the ride to work? To attract talent with this mindset, your company must impact the world or offer something to it. This is where the most investment is taking place. You must be changing the world or they lose interest.

Education Is My Passion

When I was 40 years old, I was pretty happy with my place in real estate, and my career was exactly where I wanted it to be. But as a woman in real estate in Mexico, I was happy but not satisfied. It is one thing to be happy; another thing is to be satisfied.

I wanted to help my country and give the next generation more opportunities through the power of education. I wanted a way to affect more of the world, and you can't do that without getting into education. As I began to investigate the state of higher education in Mexico and around the world, I was frustrated by how far education lagged in the context of the world's evolution. Technology was changing the way we live, travel, and work, but it wasn't affecting the way we teach and learn at the same rate.

I was disappointed to discover that universities were still dividing the right and the left side of the brain. In my opinion, that line should be erased. I don't understand this atavistic idea that numbers need to fight against creativity – this foolish notion that if you're a creative person, you cannot be a businessperson.

I went to visit the top 30 universities in the world in person. The more I studied them, the less I wanted to give my money or my time to them. I decided to open my own university with a program completely different than the ones I'd seen in the world.

I asked the president of every single university that I visited the same question: "If you were able to change one thing about this university, what would you do?"

Without fail, they each gave me the exact same answer, "Get rid of bureaucracy. Bureaucracy is killing me."

This is why the DNA of CENTRO will never be bureaucratic. We created a university with a very unconventional curriculum because it has a completely creative way of thinking. We developed a really creative economy, where 30 percent of the curriculum is business and entrepreneurship. Even if you want to study film or digital design, business entrepreneurship will be a part of your curriculum.

We have 310 professors from 26 nationalities, and every single one of them teaches part-time. To teach at CENTRO, you must also run a business. No more hiding from the economy in ivory towers for our professors. The students aspire to be like their teachers.

I can't understand why a full-time professor would be teaching entrepreneurship. It's baffling to me that someone can teach something they don't know how to do in real life.

Real entrepreneurs know what it's like to be working Thursday night and wondering if you will have any money Friday morning. It takes an iron stomach to be an entrepreneur.

We built our entire curriculum around this belief. We currently offer 800 undergraduate degrees, 18 master's degrees, and 120 continuous education programs with over 3,000 students.

At any given time, 35 percent of the students are on scholarship. That is part of my plan for improving my country. We will never say no to deserving students just because they don't come from wealthy families.

Although the opportunity to grow exists in Mexico, our strength comes from our faculty. It's very difficult to find more professors of the quality that we have here. So we intend to grow internationally, starting with the United States. We studied the market in the whole country and have decided that when we open our next campus it will be in Miami, Florida. It's still two years away, but we have already secured the site. Being in real estate, that was extremely important to me.

Unlike every other university in the United States, our classrooms do not look the same as classrooms from before the Industrial Revolution. It's ridiculous how resistant to change these well-regarded institutions are.

I am on the board at multiple universities, and the days of the professor being the all-powerful source of knowledge are over. Students can pull out their phones and find answers faster than raising their hands and asking a question.

When I went to school, the professors "knew everything," and their word was gospel. Any time a professor makes a mistake now, the students catch it by looking online. Modern professors need to realize that they have shifted roles to that of facilitators. They are there to guide the students as they learn and share their experiences and their thoughts.

At CENTRO, we don't rely on final exams that students cram for and then forget everything about the second they hand in their answer sheet. We grade our students on the process.

Life is about the process, not a final exam. If your process of life is perfect, your end result will be perfect. Nothing in our classrooms is static. We care more about what gives our students the best results and the best experience. They might sit in a circle, on the floor, or even on pillows. Adaptability is the new way of teaching.

Dalia Empower

My life changed dramatically when I finally found my "why." There are so many things you do in life without ever understanding the reason. I will never stop doing real estate because I love it, but the ability to inspire or change the life of a young person is a different reward, and it is my deepest passion.

Twenty years ago, I started a foundation for domestic violence and bullying. These behaviors are completely unacceptable to me. The foundation built high-security hospices where women and children lived with us for four months. This eventually evolved into Dalia Empower.

Nearly two decades ago, I joined an organization called The Committee of 200, which includes 200 women leaders in corporate life and in the world. We go to universities to speak to women about our lives and how we balance our corporate success.

The more I go and talk to women, the more I get frustrated to see how much is needed for them to be empowered and to know that they can achieve whatever they want.

Four years ago, the president of Mexico asked me if I would be willing to represent the women of Mexico in the G20 Initiative. At first, I wondered why he would even ask me. I'm not active in any political party, and I'm not a part of the government.

But then I realized that those were the exact reasons he reached out to me. Because I owe no allegiance to a political party, I can more freely speak about what the women in Mexico most need.

I started in Turkey, then I went to China, Berlin, and finally to Argentina. I had to draft a document for the G20 explaining exactly what the women of Mexico need. As I worked on this project, I became frustrated again. I was developing a recipe for success but without access to the right ingredients. The recipe will not work unless women find the power within themselves.

Women need to realize that they can find a balance between corporate and family life. They need to see that men can be partners in life and in business; that the only path to success is cooperation. It's not about women fighting for their rights. This is a world where men and women must live in harmony, not competition.

I decided to open the Dalia Empower schools to teach women hardcore courses on the skills they need to reach leadership positions. Women make up 55 percent of college graduates in Mexico but only 5 percent of board members.

We started this project two years ago, and we recently opened the first courses for Dalia Empower. Each class graduates 25 new women with the skills to take those board seats.

Our idea is to open franchise models in locations from Chile to Canada. When we finish that, we will cross the ocean and go to Europe. We will teach hardcore courses as well as the soft skills like "How Do You Balance Your Life," "Mindfulness," "How Do You Educate Your Children," and "Break the Glass Ceiling." These lessons are critical for women.

We are also going to teach men how to empower the women in their organizations and how to mentor them. We want men to help. So often, women complain about being excluded from male-only spaces, yet we are the first ones to exclude men. At Dalia, we believe in men and women working together.

My Advice

Women need to follow their dreams and passions and should work together with their partners, if they decide to have a partner in life. It is time to shed stereotypes. We are the architects of our own destinies.

Nobody has ever offered to build a building for me. Nobody will do my job for me in real estate. Why should I expect that in life?

Women must decide what they want to do in life and then pursue that dream. They can achieve anything they set their minds on. Nothing is impossible.

Teamwork is critical to success, whether you are a man or a woman. I lost my father when I was 11, and he was my hero. I never got on very well with my mother because she always told me that I never took no for an answer.

I always thought she was pointing out a flaw, but now I realize that it was a compliment. My refusal to take no for an answer is how I have achieved so much in my life.

Don't take no for an answer. Find the right people to help you achieve whatever you want to do.

Mentors are so important to success in the world of real estate, and yet it's so difficult to find one. If you cannot find a mentor, go to a bookstore and read biographies about people you admire; let them mentor you through their lives and actions. If you can't access a great mentor in person, you can learn a great deal from the way they lead and do business.

I did have a mentor, who didn't actively mentor me very much, but he was somebody that I admire a lot. He helped me a great deal because I observed the way he did everything. He has a perfect balance. Everyone that I admire possesses a great deal of emotional intelligence. People who possess this skill have amazing lives.

I start every day with a big breakfast, sometimes eating much more than the men around me. I also meditate every single day. It's such an amazing practice, and I'm on the board of the Global Wellness Institute, so I'd better meditate!

I work 10 to 12 hours daily, and I have 5 children. My life is defined by my ability to multitask. I always find time for my children. They are my most valuable asset.

Women should never feel guilty for not spending enough time with their families. We often discover that work and family each demand 100 percent of our time, but this much time is not available.

We all have to split our time, and guilt is a major issue with women. Do not feel guilty. It's okay to fail. When I think about failing, I believe that the minute you fail is the minute that you stop trying. The rest is just making steps toward success.

My Philosophy

Above all else, you should be honest and trustworthy. Without these elements, our society will collapse. I encourage every one of you entrepreneurs to become a philanthropist, hopefully in the early part of your careers. You must find a way to give back to the society around you. Be willing to help people in need. The help doesn't have to be financial, and those you help don't need to be strangers.

You must always work hard. There is no success without effort. My hope is that more young people will go into the entrepreneurial arena. The world needs more entrepreneurs, leaders, and role models. Our world is currently suffering from a significant lack of worthy role models. I hope that people who find inspiration from their role models can also find a way to be an inspiration for others.

Key Principles

- If you are investing in ground-up development or redevelopment projects, construction costs and timing need to become critical parts of your decision tree.

- When taking on debt, make sure you are in a strong enough financial position to endure the inevitable market shocks and downturns.

- Technology is changing real estate at an astonishing pace. Players in the industry need to be aware of these changes and try to preempt the effects on their real estate businesses.

- The driverless car will bring about a major shift in how the whole world is run and will absolutely have implications on real estate.

- Don't take no for an answer, keep working until the answer is yes. Find the right people to help you achieve whatever you want to do.

- Be honest, trustworthy, and a role model for others.

- The feeling of satisfaction and fulfillment will come when you lead a life with purpose and mission.

Exercise

Gina Diez Barroso is a true entrepreneur. One trait that is evident with Gina — and all of the other Real Estate Titans in this book — is that she looks at things differently than most people. While the average person sees how things are, she sees and envisions how they could be better. As an entrepreneur, Gina perceives risk differently than the average person because she knows that there will be many challenges and turbulent times down the road with her investments; however, she is confident that she will find a way to resolve those challenges and be successful. Gina will not allow for failure; she will get up and try again because she is so passionate about what she is doing. During my interview with Gina, I witnessed the tremendous passion in her body language and her entire presence; you can see this with all successful entrepreneurs. Gina's passion — above all else — is to make an impact; getting financially wealthy, in her view, is simply a byproduct achieving entrepreneurial success. With this in mind, I would like you to think about what part of the real estate market or segment inspires and fires you up? What is your dream and what are you currently doing that you no longer want to do? What would need to happen for you to have a tremendous zest for your business like the one Gina has?

Chapter 5

Elie Horn

Cyrela Brazil Realty
Sao Paulo, Brazil

There is no reward without risk

Elie Horn has built a real estate empire in Brazil, but he wasn't born there. As a young boy, he left Syria (Aleppo) behind for the streets of São Paulo. A devout Jew and an aficionado of contributing to the world, he has given away the majority of his money to charity.

His desire to help the less fortunate began long before most of us earned our first penny. Way back during his schoolboy days, Elie Horn was raising money to help those living on the streets in his adopted home.

He believes God brings you into the world and tests you along the way and plans on doing everything possible to pass those tests and leave the world a better place than he found it. He and his wife were the first members in South America to sign Warren Buffett and Bill Gates's Giving Pledge, promising to give away more than half of their wealth to charity. Elie Horn is truly committed to giving away wealth in ways that will help those less fortunate.

According to *Forbes*, Brazil ranks no. 8 in the world on the list of countries with the "most billionaires" and has generated 42 new billionaires worth a combined $172 billion in the past 30 years.[1] Elie Horn hopes that his decision will lead his fellow billionaires to take similar actions.

More than anything, Elie Horn's desire to give is motivated by his deep religious beliefs. As he gives away treasure in this world, he amasses it in the next. One of his greatest memories is meeting a young woman whose life he was able to save by funding her cancer surgery.

Humble Beginnings

I didn't grow up around real estate, and I certainly didn't go to school for it, but as I entered the working world, my father and brother were already in the real estate business, buying and selling apartments, so I decided to do the exact same thing. I had no idea what I was doing, but I had my father and brother to guide me.

I began buying apartments with very little money up front. I would put down 10 percent of the value in cash (equity) and borrow another 90 percent in financing from the bank. I had a 90-day window to flip each apartment I purchased, or I would be in big trouble with the bank and lose my investment. I figured that I could keep my head above water as long as I could sell the majority of the apartments.

Sometimes, I would stay up all night just to close a deal, with that 90-day clock hanging over me like the sword of Damocles. I couldn't afford to take weekends off or push meetings back. If someone wanted to negotiate a contract at 4:00 a.m., I was there at 4:00 a.m. to close the deal. Because of hard work and diligence, 90 percent of the time I was able to flip the apartment within that three-month window.

My favorite investment in my entire career was also the most profitable for my investors. It was a mixed-use property that we developed from the ground up in Rio de Janeiro, Brazil. We built apartments and an office building, and we made a profit of $18 million, which was a return on investment that can only be described as remarkable back in the 1980s. We sold 800 residential units and 1,000 office spaces very quickly.

While I'm proud of that amazing deal, there is far more to learn from a very bad deal that I did during my career. I invested in an apartment complex where we only sold two units out of 100. It was our fault because we hadn't properly assessed the demand and, quite simply, the apartments were the wrong size, and the price was too high for that specific market. Despite our best efforts, 98 percent of the units remained unsold.

Even experienced real estate players who have reached the top make mistakes. When it happens, don't let it crush you, cripple you, or cause you to quit. Instead, learn from those mistakes and make sure that you never repeat them. Without some failure, there's no success.

At the same time, without some risk it will be difficult to find high potential rewards. Real estate investment is all about risks versus the opportunities for returns (see Figure 5.1). There needs to be a potential for an upside to compensate you financially for the reality of the risks that you are taking. When you take on risks, learn to understand them all and try to mitigate as many as you can.

Curiosity is critical to success in this business. It is the fuel that leads to expertise in any area of the real estate business. At my company we might be blessed to be offered so many opportunities, but we only choose a few to move forward with. In order to make the best decision, you need to understand how viable the project is. Figure 5.2 shows a number of reasons why potential deals might never materialize.

Our business is focused on ground-up development. We look at what macro and micro issues are occurring at the moment, how much leverage we can get from the bank, the pricing of the

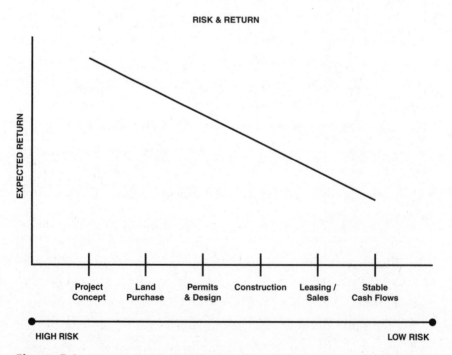

Figure 5.1 Pinpointing levels of risk and return.

DEAL FUNNEL (HYPOTHETICAL EXAMPLE)

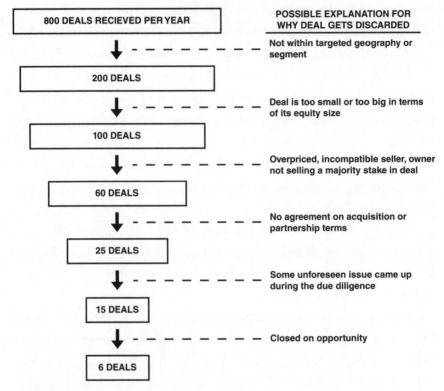

	POSSIBLE EXPLANATION FOR WHY DEAL GETS DISCARDED
800 DEALS RECIEVED PER YEAR	Not within targeted geography or segment
200 DEALS	Deal is too small or too big in terms of its equity size
100 DEALS	Overpriced, incompatible seller, owner not selling a majority stake in deal
60 DEALS	No agreement on acquisition or partnership terms
25 DEALS	Some unforeseen issue came up during the due diligence
15 DEALS	Closed on opportunity
6 DEALS	

Figure 5.2   Moving deals through a funnel to find the best ones.

deal, the costs of every single element in building (cost of steel, cement, elevators, marble, windows, etc.), the complexities of the soil and land, what we believe we can sell the apartments for when we complete the project, how fast (absorption rates) we can sell those apartments, among others. This is far from an exhaustive list of what we look at when we assess the project, but it is certainly a beginning.

When looking at a deal, and especially your first deal, analyze as much information as possible to decrease the number of mistakes that you will make. Notice that I said "decrease" and not "prevent."

Mistakes are inevitable. Your goal is to minimize the downside when those mistakes do happen. I'm glad that my mistake was with a 100-apartment deal rather than an 800-apartment deal, in which I would have lost much more money.

At the beginning of your real estate career, focus on areas of innovation; learn about new construction methods, architecture, and sales and leasing. Build a business that you can be proud of. Understand as much as you can about the way the market is shifting—the way people are looking for different types of working and living spaces, and how different pieces of technology can change everything.

Where people want to live might be entirely changed by drone delivery services, Uber, and driverless cars. Pay attention to the way the world is shifting, be forward-thinking, anticipate, and you will find true success.

Leverage is a critical part of every deal. When financing my deals, I try to find a balance. In my business, which is ground-up development, we usually leverage between 50 and 60 percent, but not beyond that because then it can become dangerous and painful. Something to remember is that best opportunities in the real estate segment are usually present when financing is most difficult to obtain.

Improving yourself as a person is a critical step on the path to success in real estate. While being a dealmaker seems like the most important part of real estate, you must also be honest, persevere, work on your intelligence, and, overall, work very hard.

As you grow and expand, keep in mind how you affect the world. Think of others and how you can make the world a better place. Money without an element of philanthropy is worthless. Do good things for others in life whenever you can. Some of my biggest mistakes came from pride, my ego, and laziness. Rather than focusing on the business, I focused too much on myself in those moments.

When people make a lot of money, they get used to a life of luxury, and that's when it is easy to become lost. Don't let success in this business destroy your focus and do not get distracted by all the glitter.

When deals are going well, it's easy to stay in a good mental state, but when things get tough, your mental fortitude will be tested. Strengthening your mind is essential. Feed your mind everyday with knowledge and inspiration.

Life is a war, and you need to know how to manage that war. God made people a certain way and gave them different qualities, so they could all be successful, but it's never linear. Change is more than just possibility; it is inevitability.

Your ability to predict what will come next that guarantees success, but rather your ability to adapt when it comes. Gird your mind so that you are ready when the time comes to adapt. I can't predict when the next shock will strike the market, or the next big change will come, but I do know that shocks and changes will come.

Keep Learning

I'm not at the end of my journey. I'm honored that some people think I'm worthy of looking up to, but I'm just a guy who got inspired by his father and brother and found a bit of success.

It's very important to have mentors and people that you can learn from. I look up to Bill Gates and Warren Buffett because they're smart, and they're the most prominent philanthropists in history. I also look up to Sam Zell because he's one of the greatest real estate players of all time.

Fitness and health are a big part of my life. You can't make the deals you need to make if you're sick in bed. Opportunity doesn't wait. I pray, go to the gym, and participate in philanthropy every single day. These are the most important routines in my life.

I spend a great deal of time reflecting and meditating on the meaning of life.

My favorite books are not about real estate, but they are about religion. I love *The Way of God* by Rabbi Moshe Chaim Luzzatto and *The Soul of Life* by Rav Chayyim of Volozhin. These books inspire me and have left a mark in my life. I encourage everyone I meet to seek knowledge outside their primary area of focus.

My Philosophy

Every decision I make in this life is guided by four critical principles:

1. Be a good person.
2. Have faith in God.
3. Work and be productive.
4. Give meaning to life.

When you look for advice and wisdom, find people who are living the way they're teaching. One of the dangers of real estate is that many people make a living from teaching about real estate rather than doing real estate. Follow the latter while you ignore the former.

Key Principles

- Before you make any investment in properties, you need to properly assess the demand for that specific product. Understand that you need to create a product for the final user or customer, not for yourself. If you don't understand demand at a profound level, you are taking on big risks.

- Working very hard, much harder than your competitors, should eventually provide rewards. No one should outwork you.

- You will make mistakes. When they happen, don't let them crush you or cause you to quit. Instead, learn from them and make sure that you never repeat them.

- Without some failure, there can be no success.

- Whatever sector of the real estate market that you are in, build a business that you can be proud of. Understand where the market is and where it's going, how people are changing their working and living habits, and whether technology will continue to drive that change.

- The world is shifting rapidly, be forward thinking, anticipate, and you will find true success.

- Leverage is a critical part of every deal. Don't use more than 60 percent financing in your deals.

- Stay humble and grounded when you succeed in real estate.

- Strengthening your mind is essential; be ready to face down-turns in your real estate career and be ready to get up when times are tough.

- When you look for advice, find people who have already been successful in whatever area it is you need advice.

Exercise

Know your market. As you've noticed, before Elie Horn makes an investment he learns the most intricate details about the market he enters. All Real Estate Titans acquire an in-depth knowledge of the selected market(s) they invest in. They stay on top of the latest market trends—such as home price and cap rate movements, pipeline of new construction, new potential infrastructure improvements in the area, main lenders and their mortgage terms, unemployment rates, and consumer spending habits, to name a few—which let real estate investors understand current conditions and plan for the future. Real Estate Titans are able to extrapolate—in many but not all cases—when trends may change and good opportunities arise.

Think about a real estate opportunity that you are analyzing and try to write down 15 important market trends that you are seeing. Think through how that will benefit or affect your potential investment.

Notes

1. www.forbes.com/billionaires/#4786f226251c.

Chapter 6

Richard Ziman

Arden Realty and Rexford Industrial
Beverly Hills, California, USA

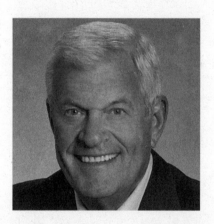

Success is about
making a difference

Known for being a real estate mogul and a philanthropist, Richard Ziman is a man who has always looked at the future. His passion for changing the world centers on education, and his mission is about passing on knowledge and creating things that last, even though buildings last a short time compared to this view of the future. For five full decades he has been defined by his admirable efforts to give back to the community in all shapes and forms. Even before he became a Real Estate Titan, Richard Ziman was investing in social causes. Investment in the world around you pays back dividends.

In recent years, things have come full circle, and now more young minds can learn about real estate at the UCLA Ziman Center for Real Estate—a powerful institute of learning funded by an endowment from Richard Ziman himself. He still sits on the boards of UCLA, as well as other universities, so that he can continue to pour wisdom gained from decades at the top of the real estate game into the next generations.

Every human has a moral imperative to make the world a better place, and this Titan lives up to that obligation. As a lifelong philanthropist, Richard Ziman has donated to many amazing causes from medical research to education around the world. Through education, anyone can be raised out of poverty and into a position where they can affect the world around them.

The Early Days

Long before the idea of real estate entered the picture, I planned to make my father proud by becoming a dentist. I attended the best dental school in the entire country, but I left after two days. After realizing the error of my choice, I decided to go to law school.

It was 1964 and a tumultuous time in the history of the United States, as the country was preparing to enter the war in Vietnam. Law school was tougher than I ever imagined. One professor in particular, to whom I will show mercy for by not mentioning his name, made my life a living hell—and I wasn't the only one he targeted. He made *our* lives a nightmare, both mentally and emotionally. The entire class was sure that he was going to get removed because of his antics, but one semester passed, and then another. One bad teacher single-handedly assassinated my passion for the law.

There was only one thing I dreaded more than dealing with him, and that was the Vietnam War. I stayed in law school not only to avoid entering the military but also to please my father, who'd sacrificed so much in his life to give me this opportunity. I didn't have it in my heart to quit on him. Instead, I decided to hit the books even harder and do whatever it took to find a way around this obstacle.

The moment I graduated from law school, I received a notice to report for the draft, which at that time was considered a death note. Once you report to your physical, you're going to get drafted, you're going to get sent to Vietnam, and you're probably going to die.

I fought against this notice. I appeared before the draft board and explained that I would not go. Two good friends of mine had already been killed over there. I was now a lawyer and while I might not have my first job yet, there was no way would I possibly go to Vietnam to follow in my fallen friends' footsteps. Amazingly, I never heard from the draft board again. To this day, I still don't know why they never came after me.

At that time of graduation, I was lucky enough to receive three different job offers. I went to work for a major law firm called Loeb & Loeb for $500 a month. At the time, my wife was making more than double that, earning $1,100 a month as a teacher.

I was researching in the library for other lawyers day and night, watching my soul get sucked out of my body month after month. Eventually, I went to the managing partner's office and said, "I don't want to do this anymore. I didn't spend seven years training to be a lawyer so that I could be a book gopher for somebody else." He did not like it, but wanted me out of his hair, so he told me one of the other lawyers needed help on a merger deal and ordered me to go help him. This was just two years after I took the bar exam.

Following my manager's order, I went to meet this lawyer. As I walked into his office, he told me he was heading off to Europe and wanted me to take care of a couple of real estate deals for him while he was away.

I'd never even taken a real estate class in law school except for entitlements, and I'd certainly never taken any business classes. But in that moment, I saw my opportunity, and I did what anyone would do in a situation like that: I faked it.

I said, "Sure, I can do it." Then I quickly called everyone I knew to find out about title insurance, mortgages, deeds and trust guarantees, and purchase and sale agreements.

Opportunities

The hardest part is getting the opportunity. The knowledge is out there. Sometimes, opportunities will come your way, and you will be tempted to turn them down because you don't know how to do what's required yet. But you can always learn. These days, it's even easier. You can find all the information you need on the internet. When I started faking my way into a real estate career, the fax machine hadn't even been invented.

I found a way to adapt and overcome. I took all the necessary forms from this lawyer and miraculously closed both deals before the end of the year. I wasn't even sworn in as a lawyer yet. I'd passed the bar, but I hadn't yet taken the oath.

Within three years, I became a partner at that law firm. It usually takes seven to nine years to become a partner. I began to explode as a real estate attorney and, within a few years, I was the largest real estate attorney in the United States.

In 1969, I had a referral from a banking client to do a REIT. At the time, these existed in the law, but nobody actually did them. We then did a $49 million IPO, which was huge money back then.

We are so used to hearing of companies valued in the billions these days that we forget just what money was worth a few decades ago. There are now Silicon Valley businesses that have never sold anything—never made $1 in profit—but investors value them at a billion dollars or more. A $49 million deal 60 years ago was astounding.

A decade later, I was convinced that I was smarter than all my clients and decided to move away from the legal part of real estate. I figured that I knew the business and everyone in it, no way could I miss. I was very wrong.

On day one, I leased a 1000-square-foot office and immediately went into contract to buy a building in Carmel, California, that I was going to turn into a timeshare.

I also bought several high-rises and about 20 apartment buildings in a complex in the luxury neighborhood of Southfield, Michigan, outside Detroit. I planned to turn all those buildings into condominiums, which was my specialty as a lawyer in Los Angeles at the time. After this acquisition, I discovered that nobody in Detroit even understood what condominium conversions were.

As a lawyer, I had represented clients in Hawaii who did this, so I figured I would find a way. I borrowed $52.5 million to acquire all these apartments. The president at that time, Jimmy Carter, saw interest rates at 5.5 percent and decided that wasn't nearly high enough. He raised them to 25 percent. So now I had a $52.5 million loan out with an interest rate that had just quintupled. I felt like my world was crashing around me. I tried to find a way to work out of that hole.

The next year, the federal government took over the very bank I borrowed all that money from. This provided an opportunity for some of my partners and me to purchase our own debt.

I purchased my own loan, eliminated my personal liability, sold off the apartments, went back to Los Angeles, and decided to just focus on office buildings.

I made a classic mistake because I thought I knew everything. I went wide. I went after different markets and different types of products at the same time. Bad idea! My past experience, relationships, and knowledge allowed me to borrow huge amounts of money, which only magnified the size of my mistake.

In 1982, I bought my first office building in Hollywood, California. I immediately flipped it and put a million dollars in my pocket. Suddenly, I knew where to focus my real estate ambitions. I bought office buildings and began to syndicate to rich friends in the San Fernando Valley, Orange County, and all across the state. By 1985, I owned 6 million square feet and controlled a company of 80 employees called the Pacific Financial Group.

If there's one thing that can be learned from my story, it's that everything that goes up can always come back down.

In 1989, two different things happened that threatened to bring my company to its knees. The first is that the Japanese came in and began to buy everything they could at a very low cap rates (very high purchase prices). Second, asbestos had become a very bad word.

One day, I was reading the right-hand column on the *Wall Street Journal*, and I discovered that Equitable Life Insurance, Prudential, and a couple of others would no longer lend to any building that had asbestos fireproofing.

That one little news item shook me to my core. I called my property manager and asked him how much asbestos property we owned. He told me that it was 25 percent of our properties.

The good news was that the Japanese were buying everything, so we sold to them. Tokyo was absolutely loaded with asbestos at the time, so they just didn't care. Over the next 16 months, I slowly eased out of and sold all of my buildings that had asbestos.

We survived, but only barely. I went from 80 employees down to just 8, and we were in the midst of a massive real estate recession by 1991.

I began to buy mobile home parks, figuring that people would do anything to stay there and that the terms could be quite generous. The government helped, but eventually, that stream of money dried up.

In 1993, again reading the *Wall Street Journal*, I discovered that Los Angeles led the country in small business formations. I saw another opportunity to get back into the office sector, so I bought office spaces significantly below replacement cost (70 percent off). I bought two office buildings, one in the Valley and one in Beverly Hills.

Just as I began to get my feet back the earthquake of 1994 hit. I saw an opportunity. While everyone was running away, I began to run toward the danger and refused to back down. When everyone else is afraid to invest, that's when you find the greatest opportunity.

A man I had done dealings with in the past—and honestly didn't like very much—approached me and told me that they had a partner who was looking for the smartest, most aggressive buyer of office space in Southern California.

We'd had a rough deal a few years earlier, and I wasn't exactly jumping at the idea of another headache. I was hesitant. I asked who he was working with, but he said it was a big secret. I had to sign a bunch of nondisclosures before he would even tell me who he wanted me to work with.

He convinced me that this was the biggest deal I would ever do. I was curious, and I decided to sign on the dotted line. His partner turned out to be Lehman Brothers.

They wanted to team up with me, but I wasn't interested. Instead, they struck a deal for me and put up 95 to 100 percent of the required equity, took on the debt, charged a certain number of points, and then gave me more depending on how aggressive they thought the loan was.

By 1995, we had 4 million square feet in 20 properties. My contact at Lehman called me to say that they wanted to take their company public, but I was skeptical. Who ever heard of taking a real estate company public during a recession? Going public is very expensive, and it's a very big financial risk.

In the end, they were able to convince me that it was the right decision, and we began the arduous preparation process. There had been no real estate IPOs for a couple of years, and there was a new rule allowing the tax-free formation of a limited partnership structure that allowed all the big old-time developers to convert their bankrupt positions into new vehicles, raise money by going public, and then go on to live another day.

The new law was passed in the early 1990s, and we were the first company to go public after its passing. Certainly, nobody was going public to start a real business at the time, but I had a feeling that we would find a way to succeed. We were exclusively based in Southern California.

We raised $430 million, paid off all of Lehman Brothers debt, and had another $430 million in public equity. With a little extra money from some other sources, we controlled $550 million in debt. We were the first of the REITs to have a bank line of that size.

With access to so much capital, we went on a buying spree. From September 1996 right up until 1999, we had 8 million square feet, and we added a transaction that added 5 million square feet to our portfolio in just that single transaction. Suddenly, we had 14 million square feet of property. By 2005, we had 20 million square feet of property under our control. We were the largest holding company in all Southern California.

Family Business

Meanwhile, I had always owned some industrial real estate. I bought my first industrial building at the age of 26, while I was still a lawyer. At that time, I brought my father into the industrial building world. He was a furniture manufacturer, which was just a small trade, and he was barely scratching out a living.

I started buying a few buildings here and there and working with my dad and my brothers. By 1995, we formalized that relationship into a family partnership between my four brothers and myself. My sister joined us later and now the five siblings, along with some of our children and grandchildren, operate that family business together. My little brother runs the assets from day to day.

The beauty of the real estate business is that you can give so many opportunities to other people. I was able to use my success in real estate to raise the rest of my family and give back to my father, who had sacrificed so much to give me opportunities, and whose love, dedication, and belief in me had kept me in law school when times were tough and I felt alone.

In 2001, as I was building this family business, I would call one of my father's childhood friends, Howard Swimmer, whenever I had questions. He was a well-known broker who mostly worked in industrial real estate. I would ask him what I wanted to know, repeat his answers to my family, and they would think I was a genius.

Mentors

In my life, there were three primary mentors. The first was my father. He was a very street-smart immigrant and an amazing human being, and he died in a car accident in 1984. I miss him very much; without his dedication and mentorship, I would never have become what I am today. My mother passed away in 1998.

The second mentor in my life was Jon Kreedman. He was a great mentor and teacher. He was a real estate developer and a client. For every deal he did, he needed two more to later bail him out. He was the living embodiment of Murphy's Law in the real estate industry. What could possibly go wrong in any deal always did for him on every third deal, and what could go right always did on the other two. He had a lot of bad luck and a crazy amount of success. Extraordinary events happened to him so often that it was a great educational process for me.

My third mentor was Arthur Gilbert. In 2001, he passed away as one of the largest individual art collectors and investors in the world. His art collection is now in London's Victoria and Albert Museum, as well as in the Gilbert Trusts and the Gilbert Foundation. Upon his death he left an additional $42 million in cash, $65 million in real estate, and 400 bank accounts insured by the bank for $100,000 each. That shows what he thought about the stock market.

He appointed me, along with a partner, as sole trustees of this massive fund. The art, which was separate, became the largest gift ever made in the United Kingdom. He donated almost $500 million in artworks. Queen Elizabeth had knighted him, and this was how he repaid her. His work can be viewed now in the finest galleries in the world, visited by over 400 million people every single year.

The remaining trust controlled $150 million in the marketable securities and alternative investments. Through alternative investments, my partner and I elevated the trust to become one of the most sophisticated and respected foundations working in education, health, and cultural support. With 27 programs in Israel and 4 in Berkeley in the north, the rest of it is mostly in the south, mainly at UCLA, but also in The Hebrew University in Jerusalem. We also have programs at the City of Hope—a world-class cancer facility in suburban Los Angeles, where I was chairman for a time.

Finding the Perfect Deal

Different investments are useful for different reasons. Buying a home for $300,000 and selling it 8 years later for $3 million is a good deal. Buying a home for $89,000 and selling it 10 years later for a million bucks is a good deal too. It all depends on whether you're making a deal for money or you're buying real estate for your family and setting down personal roots.

There's no one deal that's *the* great deal to look for. Your goals for good investments should depend on your strategic position. Your goal in real estate is to have a lot of good deals. You'll have some major scores along the way, and you want to avoid having too many bad deals. We've all got them, and you should expect them as part of this process. Without risk, there's no reward.

I believe that there are four major factors to success in real estate. The first two are timing and location, but location is not as important as timing. That's because it's rare for someone to buy a bad location. If you're buying a property, you should think the location is okay at minimum, but when you buy that property and eventually sell it or refinance it, it will be all about timing. When you buy will determine when you sell and how good you do.

The third factor is debt timing. Whether your interest rate is 3 or 7 percent, whether it's a 60 or 80 percent loan, it's all about the timing.

The fourth essential factor for success in real estate is to understand demand. Sooner or later, demand dictates everything. It will generate financing availability. It will fill vacancies and ultimately push up rents. When you have no demand, you run into vacancies, you can't pay your mortgage, and then you're in trouble. Every single issue is affected by demand, so be patient and analyze. Look at all the factors that generate demand. The availability of financing, the status of the economy, GDP growth in your city or state, job formations, inventory in the market—much of this information is in the *Wall Street Journal*. Look at any tax reform news, the stock market—put them all together, and that will tell you the demand. The greatest mistake you can make in real estate is not understanding about demand.

When a deal seems too good to be true, we make too many promises to lenders and investors and take on too much debt, and that can shatter us.

You need to have the right mindset. You need to believe in your own ability and believe that you are making the correct decisions. Be open to critics and be willing to learn from others. During downtimes, your mindset is crucial. When times get tough, it's absolutely critical to believe in yourself.

Above anything else, always make sure you take care of your physical and mental health. You want to build deep, strong family, friend, and associate relationships. Pick a trade that you know you'll be good at. Become involved in sports and outside activities that can help you interact in a social and charitable life.

Key Principles

- When opportunities come knocking on your door, if you have very little to lose, you should take them even if you are not ready for them.
- Understand where interest rates are and where experts think they are going, especially if you live in an emerging market or take on a loan with a floating interest rate.

- When you're just getting started in real estate, it's best to focus on one region and one type of property to develop a depth of knowledge, relationships, and skill.

- Your best investments will likely come when you buy during downturns and market softenings, when most of your competitors won't be purchasing real estate.

- If you are successful in real estate, the great thing is that you can help other people and give them opportunities.

- Mentors can be very important guiding forces to your success and save you from making bad business decisions.

- Your goal in real estate is to have a lot of good deals and to avoid having many bad deals.

- The four major factors for success in real estate are (1) choosing a good location, (2) good timing of your acquisition, (3) correct timing of your debt obtention, and (4) understanding demand.

- During downtimes, your mindset is crucial. When times get tough, it is absolutely critical to believe in yourself.

Exercise

Richard Ziman understands, at a very prominent level, that when there is a high demand for properties in a particular neighborhood or city coupled with a lack of supply of quality properties, prices will rise. When there is little or no demand for these properties due to a weak economy—or another reason—there will be an oversupply of properties and prices will fall. With this essential principle in mind, I would like you to analyze the main demand drivers for a property that you are looking to invest in. If you don't have a property, think about a potential opportunity in the neighborhood you live in. Here are some demand drivers to analyze: the increase or decrease in population and employment in the neighborhood or trade area, redevelopment growth (replacing outdated real estate), relocation growth (relocation changes due to neighborhood perception), studying the history of the economy in that specific neighborhood or city, understanding which parts of the city are growing fastest, what new companies have been opening offices or warehouses and where, what new infrastructure is being built or developed, what are the demographics like and what is the average age of the population, what percent of the population has smartphones and access to internet, and how far away your property is from services (schools, hospitals, public transportation).

Chapter 7

Robert Faith

Greystar
Charleston, South Carolina, USA

Real estate is an entrepreneurial business

When it comes to southern hospitality, there is no greater example than Robert Faith—a man who dresses casually for work and runs an office with few walls, smiling often and allowing his team at Greystar to collaborate in a fun and effective environment.

Originally destined to follow his father's footsteps to become a petroleum engineer, Bob Faith's path took a hard-left turn over 30 years ago, as he went on to create one of the world's largest rental housing investment, development, and management groups.

With his freshly printed engineering diploma in hand, he entered a job market with no opportunities (due to the recession of the early 1980s). Like many young entrepreneurs, he decided to quickly exit the job market and continue his education: the perfect way to avoid the recession.

He went to Harvard Business School. After graduating with his MBA, Bob was able to find work at one of the largest property development firms in the country, Trammell Crow, which had a penchant for hiring fresh MBAs from elite business schools around the country and throwing them to the wolves. The great would rise to the top, while the merely good ones would sink to the bottom.

At the time, Trammell Crow was cleaning up the disaster left behind by the savings and loan scandal, which had become a crisis. His first assignment was to help his new employers exit the troubled projects left behind.

Even at the start of his career, he demonstrated a liking for finding solutions to the most complicated of Gordian knots. Knowing that he could always find a solution, Bob demonstrated contagious positivity and became renowned as a morale booster.

By the end of the decade, Bob had helped Trammell Crow in myriad endeavors and was ready to create his own company.

In 1991, he formed an alliance with a friend from his Harvard days named Barry Sternlicht to form Starwood Capital. Twenty-four months later Bob decided to create Greystar.

In His Own Words

People think of real estate as something solely controlled by big players, but nothing could be further from the truth. The world is filled with land. No matter where you're standing, you're surrounded by land. Real estate is still a very fragmented market, and that means it is very entrepreneurial.

While there are some big players with massive funds, there are also millions of deals that are too small to interest them. Investors focused on giant high rises in New York are not going to flip single-family homes in a small town in the middle of America. It's outside their expertise and, financially, the deal is too small for them. That leaves a great deal of opportunities for those new to the real estate game.

I've always had an entrepreneurial itch. I began my real estate career at Trammell Crow, a world-class organization. Working at a company like this, you can be an "intrepreneur," meaning you are an entrepreneur within a large organization that surrounds and supports you. Starting there was priceless and taught me so much.

Back in the 1980s, when I graduated from Harvard Business School, a company could borrow from a financial institution up to 105 percent of the development cost. The extra 5 percent was just so we could pay ourselves. That business plan lasted until the savings and loan crisis of the early 1990s hit, smashing just about everyone and stalling the entire US market.

We were able to get so much leverage for our first deals, whether they were distribution centers or speculative. But then, suddenly, after the crisis of 1991, we had to get equity investments.

Whenever there is a market shift, the real estate market enters the phase of "adapt or die." We had no choice but to adapt. I had to raise private money, which was something new for me. We could no longer raise all of our money from the bank. The banks were tighter in response to this crisis, and that caused me to form a new company called Starwood Capital Partners with my old classmate Barry Sternlicht.

Together, we raised equity and started buying properties. Our very first deal together was a warehouse building. While at Trammell Crow, we had a long-term deal with AT&T, and I knew some people there, so my first deal was to team up with them to lease this warehouse.

Back in my Starwood days, when we were liquidating assets, we had an apartment complex in Tampa, Florida, called River Gardens. We were so excited to discover that the property was going up for auction. When the time came to bang the gavel, only single-family homebuyers showed up. We sat through over 200 auctions of single-family homes. And then the River Gardens property came up.

Our standard auction policy was to never bid first. We always waited to see someone else's opening bid. As the apartment complex came up on the block, we sat there waiting for someone else to make the opening bid so that we could follow. Nobody raised a paddle.

Looking around the room, we realized that no one else had the money to bid on a property of this size. The first bid was $50,000 on a property that we thought was worth $5 million. People started getting together and pooling their resources, trying to get in on this fantastic opportunity, but in the end, we swooped in and grabbed it for just $500,000—10 percent of what we felt the property was worth.

There are some "once in a lifetime" opportunities when you have the government forcing a liquidation ahead of the market.

My favorite deal is always the last one that I've completed. It's so exciting to be in the middle of every single transaction. Earlier this year, we acquired and privatized EdR, one of the nation's largest developers, owners, and managers of high-quality collegiate housing communities, in a $4.6 billion transaction.

Sweat Equity

People often ask how I was able to raise money in 1991 when no one else could—when everyone else was shrinking because of the real estate crisis.

Fortunately, I had a friend from business school who managed some of the money for the Vanderbilt family. His strategy was to bring in money and meet someone who knew an industry and was willing to sweat and do the hard work.

I started off as the sweat equity partner, which is what anyone entering the real estate business can do—find amazing deals that they could never acquire on their own and bring them to investors. Putting in the hard work, grinding, and organizing a deal are things that have value.

My friend from business school put up the bulk of capital for us, and we were off to the races. In a weird way, having no track record at the time was actually a good track record because everyone else in the entire industry had a bad track record due to the 1991 recession.

We were very fortunate to have a partner who believed in counter-cyclical investments. He understood the value of moving in and buying when everyone else was moving out and selling. Don't follow the crowd if you want to be successful. Instead, take the road less traveled.

The Denver Downsides

We had one crazy development deal in Denver where we learned an important lesson about guaranteeing costs before you have all the details and construction documents in place. We were in a situation where we had to close on a deal or lose the land forever. In this deal, we had to guarantee the cost of the building to our equity partner or we would lose them. We ended up doing the deal, stuck in the middle, in a very vulnerable position. I fell into a common trap, and it wasn't the first time. I would often overvalue the importance of getting any specific deal done, forgetting that there's always another deal around the corner.

Recently, we were back in Denver, where we were forced to sell a property for $7 million less than what it cost us to build it. We took our hit, held a meeting, and learned from our mistake.

One of the other important lessons I've learned from my Denver disasters was to always lean toward a safer capital structure and to not take on too much leverage. I pass on deals that have too much risk because we spend more of our time trying to understand the potential risks and downsides of any transaction. A great deal is less about having an amazing upside than it is about minimizing the downside.

This mindset weeds out the bad outcomes. "No risk, no reward" is true, but real estate success is about managing risk. When you're looking at doing your first deals, it's easy to get caught up in that same emotion that strikes me every time I set foot in Denver.

Even if you follow the principles in this book and get valuable advice from your local mentor, take a moment to step away from the emotion of the deal. Try to reactivate the objective part of your mind. Look at any potential downsides. What happens if this deal goes wrong? How could this deal go wrong?

Never think that a deal can't fail because there are things that are outside our control. The way we manage risk is by entering deals where we seek to minimize the downside if the deal collapses. When you manage the downside, the upside will always take care of itself.

When analyzing that risk, here are a few factors to look at: Are there any environmental issues? Is the market demand there? Can I raise equity for that specific deal? Can I raise debt? What are interest rates? What is the credit risk of my counterparty? Are there any governmental issues?

These are just some of the downside elements, but it's far from being a comprehensive list. Every state has different laws, and these laws are constantly changing. Tax laws and capital gains laws can shift in a way that could put you in a very vulnerable position if you don't stay on top of your risk management.

Adding Value

For every deal, there must be some story about the value add that will generate returns. That value add can be several things: a certain demographic change in the city, something about the building, a micromanagement supply issue, an undervalued asset to replacement cost, etc.

Find out the value creation story. No matter if you are buying a single-family home as an investment or a multibillion-dollar industrial portfolio. How and why will this property go up in value once you take control? You need to know and believe in that story.

I'm a huge believer in studying demographics and understanding their impact on demand. Many people in the US economy made money following the baby boomers. But now the market is filled with Millennials, and they are driven by different needs and desires.

The old and the young are both huge demographic sectors that affect their environments very differently. They have different types of desires and different perspectives on renting versus owning. They also have access to different amounts of capital. Before investing in any property, I would make sure to understand the demand from those two segments in your market.

Research should always track demographics. I circle back to that often because it's the central element of my thesis when we do ground-up development. Keep track of which cities are growing in population and the income levels that support that growth. For example, as of early 2018, Dallas, Austin, Nashville, and Seattle are all seeing massive population growth; however, only through research and tracking of the demographics can we determine if these cities can sustain and support that growth.

It's essential to consider supply and demand. The availability of real estate and the number of people who want that real estate controls the value and determines your ability to turn a deal into profit. Sometimes, you'll want to step away from a deal even if demand is great.

The real estate business is very cyclical. There's a lot of demand and then there's a lot of supply, then there's a lot of demand, and then there's a lot of supply. The market goes up, and then it goes down. The value of properties goes up, and then goes down. There seems to be some type of recession or crisis in every single decade. Junk bonds, savings and loans, the Great Recession—these things happen cyclically. And yet, large sectors of the market somehow seem to be surprised every time.

The challenge of the real estate business's cyclicality can become your opportunity. Most of the business with Trammell Crow was built around development, but during downturns, development is the first thing that came to a halt. Trammell learned from this and began to go into the services business.

I started in 1986 in Oklahoma and quickly realized that if we didn't focus on service in addition to development, we were going to go out of business. By preparing for the cyclicality of the real estate market, one can surpass all the companies that are surprised when the market has a downturn every decade. This preparation and adaptability strategy will allow you to stay in this business for the long-term.

Greystar is the largest operator of rental housing in the world with over 14,000 team members globally. In the housing crisis of 2008, we cruised through that down cycle because we focused on rehabbing buildings, recreating parking lots, providing services, and on asset and property management. That allowed us to be one of the early developers to break through the recession.

In this cyclical business, many of our competitors go bust because they don't think about the downturns.

This brings me back to debt. Never take recourse risk or, if you are willing to take on this massive risk, set aside the money in order to cover you. Build a resilient strategy.

Additional Advice

The leaner a business's overhead is the better. Rental housing has vast rent rolls with many tenants. No single tenant moving out will cause any serious trouble, whereas single-tenant assets have much greater risk.

If you only have four tenants in your quadplex, losing one of them costs you 25 percent of your monthly revenue. If you only have two tenants, one of them is half of your monthly revenue. This is an example of maintaining and managing the downside. "What happens if one tenant moves out?" It's a reasonable question to ask when managing the risk of a property.

Our personal debt strategy is to have 65 percent of costs with an internal cap of 75 percent maximum. There are people who've made a lot of money using higher percentages of debt, but that's the level of risk that I am comfortable with based on my experience.

As much as real estate is about demographics, markets, and finding great deals, the analytical side is critical. This means a solid understanding of finance and numbers, so that you can instantly understand the financial impact of every single decision you make.

One of the greatest skills you can hone and develop is the ability to form relationships and build a network. Combine great optimism and excitement with each new person you meet with a realistic view about the downside potential of each deal.

Study the downside of any deal you're thinking about. Real estate is exciting, and it's an opportunity to make a great deal of money, but if there is a part of you that never wants to do a deal, then you shouldn't do deals.

The Greystar recruitment process is not rocket science. Sure, we're looking for people that are bright enough, but after that, all we look for is nice people. Nobody wants to work with people they don't like, and nobody wants to do deals with people they don't like.

In life and business, if you're a nice person with a sense of integrity, you can achieve success. Being nice and treating other people well is an effective life strategy. When they like you, people will go out of their way to help you succeed. How simple is that?

Although I can share loads of financial advice and the strategies I follow, these are different for every market. The strategy for purchasing single-family homes is different than the strategy for buying parking lots. But what stays the same is that all deals are about relationships.

When you have integrity, and you're nice to people, you might not be the highest bidder or the most experienced person, but sometimes, that "once in a lifetime" opportunity will come your way.

This process begins with thinking about your customers, their needs, and their desires. What do they want? The people living in your apartments and your properties are not just numbers on a spreadsheet. They're human beings with families, children, bills, medical needs, hopes, and dreams. And they matter. When forming deals and building out your business strategy, always think about what your customers want.

Come from a place of empathy; focus on making every deal a win for the other person, and you will experience great success. It's not about winning every deal and crushing the competition. People with that mindset don't last very long.

We're living through interesting times. We're just beginning to see the tiniest impact of how technology will alter and change real estate. We can't ignore it; we need to commit to being quick and able to respond to changes in technology. Changes are not fatal, so do not be the last person waving your fist at change. Instead, think about why this change is occurring and what people will need in response to this change.

Success in this business requires long-term thinking. Balance both technical skills and a strong mindset, and that means you need to believe in yourself. When things get tough, it's easy to start thinking you don't have what it takes. Do not let that thought enter your mind.

Career Advice

A great way to get into real estate is exactly how I started—working in a company and learning the business. Work hard, network, and put yourself in a position to see and pursue opportunities. Not every real estate success story starts the same way, but for me, there is great value in learning from inside the security and structure of a company.

As an investor, you want to make sure that you're backing someone who already has some type of experience. You can read books, go to courses and seminars, and watch videos online, but the truth is, you're only going to learn in the real world. School simply cannot teach you what you'll learn in real deals. You have to go out and execute; developing your own ground-up training in the business is critical.

Mentors

Role models and mentors are important. I can't say this enough. One of my great mentors was Trammell Crow. He was a role model because of his humble culture, his openness, and the way he valued relationships and people. He did not have a fancy office in the corner. He always had a normal desk in the bullpen like everyone else, so if you wanted to go talk to him, you could. He wasn't hidden in a two-acre office behind a dozen secretaries. He was right there in the trenches next to us.

Ronald Terwilliger is another great mentor of mine, and I'm flattered to have his name next to mine in this book. He's one of the most gifted risk managers in the world. He has amazing insight on how to think about balancing overhead leverage and all the other parts of this business.

It's possible that Trammell put a little too much trust in his people. While he taught me about relationships, Ronald was my teacher on the practical side.

Surround yourself with role models and mentors who give you feedback and advice. But real mentorship doesn't come from words. Watch these people and take time to think about what you see them doing. Read other people's stories and learn what they did right and what they did wrong. I would love for this chapter to only be full of my successes, but my mistakes are where you have the greatest opportunity to learn.

Always think about what you're learning and find ways to adopt it into your own business plan. The world belongs to those who read. I am an avid reader, and I try to consume as much information about the real estate industry as possible. I am always looking for ideas from any industry that can be successful. I often learn more from reading about Apple than I do from reading about real estate.

My Philosophy

While understanding the core principles of real estate is important, there is more to the newspaper than the open houses section, and there's more to the library than the real estate aisle. Look for ideas from other industries and draw parallels on your own situation. This is how you can develop an advantage and bring a new idea to your market without having to think of that new idea.

One of my favorite books is *Results That Last* by Quint Studer. He's a healthcare consultant who helps companies improve their operations. When I read that book, it gave me great foundational ideas about how Greystar needs to address our property management business. I also love the Bible because it's a great book about how to treat people and be successful.

In addition to exercising your mind and your spirit, physical health is important. The real estate business involves a great deal of walking, from touring properties to walking into auctions. You are on your feet a lot, and if you are in poor health, you can get left behind and miss a critical piece of information or show up late to that critical bid.

I strive to maintain a balance between career and spirituality. I love to spend time in nature—fishing and hunting or just going for a walk with the dog. Spending time with your family is critical because it helps you maintain that balance. We're not automatons; we can't only live by work.

You need to replenish your spirit by spending time doing things that make you feel good. And they don't have to be expensive. Notice that none of my hobbies cost a great deal of money.

Finally, be kind. Live a life balanced between physical, mental, and spiritual. Value relationships and resist the temptation to work all the time. People are worth more than money, and they'll be there for you in the ways that matter, so you need to be there for them in the ways that matter. No matter how much success you find, high school basketball, family dinners, and ballet recitals are just as important as any deal—no matter how big its upside.

Key Principles

- Always be open to change and to listening to different perspectives. And make a point to challenge your own assumptions.

- Entrepreneurship always starts with a change in the environment. You have to look at how the world is changing and make new plans, taking advantage of those changes rather than being intimidated by them.

- Never fall in love with your asset or investment; fall in love with your investors and your stakeholders.

- Understand the value of moving in and buying when everyone else is moving out and selling. Don't follow the crowd if you want to be very successful. Instead, do things when most of your competitors are not.

- Always lean toward a safer capital structure and do not take on too much leverage. A great deal is mostly about understanding and minimizing the downside and less about analyzing the upsides.

- Learn how to analyze demand by understanding the demographics of the trade area in which you are making an investment.

- The real estate business is very cyclical. There's a lot of demand and then there's a lot of supply. The market goes up, and then it goes down. There seems to be some type of recession or crisis every single decade.

- Being a nice person and treating other people well is an effective real estate and life strategy. People want to do business with people they like, and if people like you they will go out of their way to help you succeed.

- Come from a place of empathy; focus on making every deal a win for all parties involved. Don't focus on getting everything in a deal. People with that mindset don't last very long.

- When things get tough, it's easy to start thinking you don't have what it takes. Remember that you do have what it takes to succeed: that mindset is essential.

- Surround yourself with great mentors and role models who give you advice. Watch these people and take time to think about what you see them doing.

- Try to exercise your mind, your spirit, and your body often.

Exercise

Real estate is a people's business and a strong network provides support and creates opportunities for real estate investors. An elite group—with great mentors, potential investors and business partners, friends, and more—creates an ambiance of support but also important are individuals who will challenge your ideas and help you become a better businessperson. The very best real estate investors understand the importance of building a network because much of real estate investing relies on experiential learning. What group have you wanted to join for a long time but for some reason haven't become a member of yet? Look for an elite group of people that can raise your standards and help you in your future business endeavors. Depending on your sector and personal goals, some great groups could be the Urban Land Institute, Young Presidents Organization, Entrepreneurs´ Organization, The National Association of Realtors, Boma, and ICSC, among many others.

Chapter 8

Chaim Katzman

Gazit-Globe

Tel Aviv, Israel

The sky is not falling

Every time there is a shift in the market, there is a rush to be the first to proclaim that the "sky is falling." In the real estate business, one only needs to look at the investors running around screaming about the "death of retail" to see that it's happening again.

Right now, online business accounts for 2.5 percent of the United States GDP. That sounds like a significant number until you look at the mail order business, which accounted for more than 5 percent of the GDP just a century ago.

Every new startup in Silicon Valley talks about how it will disrupt the market as though disruptions were only invented in the past decade. They weren't. Although Sears and Montgomery Ward began as mail order companies in the late 1800s, by 1930 they had stores across the country. Despite the massive success of their mail order sales business, people still love the customer experience.

According to Chaim Katzman, every big trend initially seems to change the world, and we often call it a disruption. Eventually, it slows down or disappears altogether. It becomes a part of the human experience, but things tend to return to equilibrium. A catalog can no more replace the shopping experience than a webpage. There is something that we love about going out of our homes and into a social environment to shop.

When VHS was developed it allowed consumers to enjoy the quality of a movie in their own homes. The naysayers screamed that it was the end of cinema. They were proven wrong; movies are more successful than ever. Even in the era of digital downloads and 4K video, people enjoy the experience of leaving home to enjoy a movie.

Disruption has always existed and while it may kill a single retailer, such as Blockbuster, it is rarely enough to destroy an entire market. Airbnb hasn't caused the end of the hotel industry any more than Uber has ended personal car ownership and taxis.

There is no reason to believe that retail will suddenly disappear.

Starting Out

I began my career as a real estate attorney, and as I worked with clients I became fascinated with the idea of owning an asset and the ability to create something from scratch when you do ground-up development.

My foray into real estate began in Israel, where I focused on doing a land assemblage. I purchased several connected pieces of real estate from different families and created a larger property. That initial project taught me that sometimes in real estate, 1 plus 1 can add up to 3. One of the ways to succeed in real estate is through land assemblages and creating a large irreplaceable plot of land.

The success of my first project led me to focus on assembling land for more of my initial deals. Creating larger properties allows you to enjoy some interesting arbitrage as well. The larger single property is worth more than the individual properties were, even before you begin a development.

When looking on my career, it's hard to pick out a single deal as my favorite. Each deal and property is special in its own way, but there are some properties that contain wonderful memories. I have fond memories of the property where I taught my younger brother how to drive. I love every asset we have acquired or developed, whether it was in Israel, Europe, the United States, Brazil, or Canada. When it comes to real estate you should like all your assets.

With any potential deal or project it's easy to become distracted by the glamour of the potential upside. It's far more enjoyable to focus on what you could make than on what you could lose. I had some tough experiences along the way when I attempted to venture outside my core business of real estate. I purchased a construction company, which I mistakenly thought was close enough to real estate to be manageable. The two businesses are quite different, and I failed.

I learned a valuable lesson: Stick to what you know. When you think you are smart enough to do everything, you start failing. I have never lost money in a real estate investment.

As a lawyer, I knew how to perform thorough due diligence, and this is important. You must review all legal documents, find the correct fiscal structure, and get title insurance for the property. If you are looking to do ground-up development, check the environmental and soil issues; find out if your neighbors will be a major barrier or supporter of your project.

Whenever a new opportunity is presented to me, I begin by looking at the location and the potential for what I could build there. I ask myself several critical questions; here are a few.

1. What is the state of the market that surrounds the property?
2. Does it sit on a main avenue where I can have good entry and exit points?
3. How complicated is the zoning?
4. Are the neighbors friendly or problematic?
5. Are you getting in the way of an ecosystem of that submarket?
6. What are the main risks and how can I mitigate them?
7. Do the financials make sense?
8. Do I think a financial institution will lend me money?

Trends in the Marketplace

The market is shifting with new changes in technology. If I were starting over right now, I would take a hard look at the possibilities with blockchain. There have been a few recent ICOs that focused on real estate, but this space is wide open right now. I expect great things to happen in this space in the near future, but my lack of knowledge holds me back.

Governments may step in and regulate the space while introducing their own currencies. We may be using cryptodollars, cryptoeuros, and cryptoshekels in the near future. The major risk with blockchain is that someone else could come up with a better idea.

I think that is the biggest risk. But it is definitely a space that will grow exponentially.

If I were starting out and focused on physical real estate, I would get a real estate brokers license or become a real estate property manager to learn the real estate business from the inside.

There are so many interesting pockets and niches all over. The residential space in general is always interesting, especially in rapidly growing markets where demand outweighs supply.

The public securities market is very efficient, so while it's a good investment for some people, I would not pursue that niche. I would go to where the opportunities are inefficient and where there is a lot of potential upside.

If the market is efficient the upside is going to be smaller. Financing can seem complicated when you first enter the world of real estate, but according to the rule of thumb, when most financial entities are not willing to lend you money, it's a good time to use leverage. In real estate it's good to be a contrarian. Banks will want to lend you money when the market is at the peak, but, ideally, you can get financing when the market is going through a softening or a recession because you should be able to buy or develop an asset at a better price or similar to replacement cost.

I would recommend using 50 percent leverage, although this percentage can vary depending on the asset class and geography.

Disruption

I'm constantly asked about disruption in the real estate market and it's not something that I worry about. Disruption has been around for the last 5000 years. Of course some real estate will suffer more than others. I am mostly in the retail space market, and it is likely that my Class C shopping centers in the suburbs and small towers will suffer.

However, the Class A malls, like Aventura near Miami or King of Prussia near Philadelphia, will be around for decades to come.

It's all about omni channeling, which is about providing your customers with a seamless shopping and customer service experience. The shopping journey might start in the home, whether through a catalog or a website, but it will finish in a physical location.

Fifty years ago, 80 percent of the needs of the family was found and bought inside the supermarket. Today, only 50 percent of those needs are inside the supermarket. Times have changed and companies need to evolve.

If we look at the hotel space, Airbnb has been a major disruptor, but we will always have hotels. These disruptors are something positive for the different real estate industries to evolve and improve. Real estate is about adapting to disruptions, not running away from them.

Words of Wisdom

To succeed in the world of real estate requires patience, good common sense, and the ability to understand where things are going (because sometimes it is not obvious). You must have the stomach and the hunger to get you through the tough times, because they always come. This business requires hard work, but it is a long-term business.

One thing that worries me about new investors is that they often follow the flavor of the day. They want to be the first one to jump on board a new trend. They throw money into that specific hot thing that everyone is pursuing, and then they suffer. Unfortunately, it is hard for the average investor to not follow the trend. There are always compelling reasons to invest. But if you follow what is very popular, the odds will not be in your favor. You need to think long-term, and you need to think differently.

Technical skills and knowledge are not enough to rise to the top. Believing in yourself is absolutely essential. You need to have conviction. Technical skills you can hire or outsource, and while these are important, mindset is the one thing that cannot be purchased. You must have great faith in yourself if you want to be successful in real estate.

Find mentors and guides to help you on your journey. When I began my career there were two developers in Israel that I worked for, and I learned so much from them. It was many years ago but they provided really good guidelines. The most important thing I learned from them is that patience is a big virtue in this business. The unexpected will happen and when it does, you must be patient.

My favorite book is the Bible. I don't have too many strict routines, the only guarantee every day is that I go to work. Other than that, it's hard for me to maintain a specific routine.

My final three pieces of advice are to (1) gain as much knowledge in your area of expertise as possible to achieve a competitive advantage, (2) trust in yourself and don't let other trends convince you to do otherwise, and (3) be patient. Success in real estate requires patience.

Key Principles

- Disruptions have always been around. They come and go, but things always return to equilibrium.

- Retail will not disappear, it will simply change, and tenants will have to provide better physical and online experiences.

- Sometimes in real estate 1 plus 1 can add up to 3. One of the ways to succeed in real estate is through land assemblages and creating a large irreplaceable plot of land.

- Develop a core strategy in real estate and maintain your focus there. The development and construction businesses are not the same. When you think you are smart enough to do everything, you start failing.

- The market is shifting with new changes in technology. Blockchain should become an interesting segment that we should look out for.

- Technical skills you can hire or outsource. Although these are important, mindset is the one thing that cannot be purchased. A powerful mindset is essential.

Exercise

Gazit-Globe is a public company specializing in supermarket-anchored urban shopping centers. Do you currently invest in real estate public companies? If not, do some research on this topic and analyze the potential pros and cons sheet of making an investment in a company like Gazit. If you proceed to invest in public real estate companies, what could be the potential downside if you're wrong?

Chapter 9

Rohit Ravi
Appaswamy Real Estate
Chennai, India

Find the supply and demand imbalance

The Maldives is one of the most beautiful places on earth, consisting of almost 1200 islands. As a nation originally led by kings and queens, these islands came to prominence as the perfect stop on the way to India from Europe.

Nestled to the southwest of Sri Lanka, this island nation is a slice of paradise. After the influence of colonial powers began in the sixteenth century, the people of this beautiful island chafed under the rule of various European colonial leaders until finally shaking free of British rule in 1965. The British maintained an air base on the island for another 12 years, but with their departure, this nation has begun rebuilding its reputation as the ultimate global vacation destination.

With an aim to expanding beyond fishing and traditional tourism, the Maldives have entered the twenty-first century with an eye toward luxury tourism. That's where our next Titan, Rohit Ravi, has managed to develop one of the most awe-inspiring hotels in the world, the St. Regis Vommuli Resort.

The Foundation

Real estate is in my blood. My family has been involved in real estate development ever since my grandfather founded the company in 1959, at a time when there was no organized player in southern India. At the time, the real estate market was quite fragmented, and he saw an opportunity to bring organization and structure to the market.

He began by purchasing 125 acres near the Chennai airport. Since that time, the company has built 12 million square feet and 12,000 apartments.

After building so many permanent homes and gaining a strong focus in the residential market in southern India, we began to realize that there is a great opportunity in the hotel market. When it comes to building and developing them, hotels and apartments have many similarities. Twenty years ago, we realized that it was the logical progression for our development projects, so we started experimenting with developing and investing in hotels.

Because real estate was the family business, my entrance into that world was expected; my love affair with the power of construction began at an early age.

I grew up curious about what my father did and how he took care of us. That curiosity turned into a passion, which turned into my career. Not everyone is fortunate enough to be born into a real estate legacy. There are certain pieces of knowledge passed down in families like mine, and the lessons we take for granted are difficult to learn without a mentor in your life. There are some very important real estate principles that I intend to pass on to my children and to their children after.

My company has been very successful because we follow a very simple principle: we stick to what we know in terms of asset classes and geography. We stick to a very small sector within real estate, but what we do, we do to the best of our ability, and we provide a lot of safety for our investors and developers because we have a strong name. We always try to over-deliver on our promises, and this continues to raise the value of our family name and brand.

In real estate, as in many other businesses, there is often the opportunity to gain short-term profit with a bit of deviousness. For example, some players will try to slip clauses into a contract in the hopes that the other party won't notice or won't point out that a property has damages or governmental issues. While this can earn you a little money in the short-term, eventually your reputation will get tarnished. There is nothing worse than having a former business associate or investor of yours speaking bad about you all over town. The real estate industry is very small; all the players in the local market know each other. The short-term benefits are not worth it. Your reputation should come above all else. There is nothing more valuable than your reputation—it's worth more than gold.

Developing an Island

My favorite real estate deal is one that I fully oversaw, the St. Regis Vommuli Resort in the Maldives. I learned some painful yet critical lessons there. The main one is about cost overruns. When you're developing in an exotic location or even a place that you don't know as well, big surprises will come your way. In the case of the Maldives, the destination is hard to reach. Everything is different when access and airlift is difficult.

When building on an island, the raw materials must be brought in by boat. When transporting by boat, you are vulnerable to a whole new range of surprises. Rain doesn't stop the trucks from operating when you have roads, but it can certainly turn the seas into a hazard and delay deliveries by days or even weeks when you are using water to transport materials.

A single storm can shatter your project calendar. The construction materials don't arrive on time, and you have an entire crew sitting around doing nothing for days, simply waiting for a delivery of cement or wood. Additionally, the price of raw materials can spike beyond initial projections because of the exorbitant shipping costs linked to storms and other natural unforeseen events. The number of ships operating in exotic locations is quite limited.

Our family invested heavily in this project putting up $125 million of its own equity. This wasn't nearly enough money to build something so luxurious in such a remote location. We obtained additional construction financing from a financial institution.

Much to my disappointment, the project was not completed on time. The unexpected challenges of building in the Maldives overwhelmed our meticulous planning. This put a great deal of pressure on my family. An important lesson here is that when you are in real estate development—no matter how well you plan things out—there will be things that will be out of your control.

Any time you have construction financing in place, you have interest costs that get triggered, and your investors get upset. When you're doing a deal of this size and you're late, an apology to the bank or to other stakeholders isn't enough to cover it. It's a brutal lesson; while profits grow with scale, so do the risks. And this was a very large project indeed.

Despite all these issues, in the end, the hotel opened and has had very successful operation history. Fortunately, we have won numerous awards from UNESCO, as well as the World's Leading Luxury Island Resort at the 24th World Travel Awards, a British Society award, and an SBID International Design Award, among others.

Winning awards is nice, but it's important to stay humble and ensure the stakeholders do well. As I look back on this experience, I wish going in that we'd known a little better what we learned on the other side. Whenever you invest in a new location, new surprises will arise, and local knowledge can be incredibly valuable. In this situation we lacked a little bit of that local knowledge.

For this reason, it's better to focus your real estate projects in a region you fully understand and know. While two-story houses might be quite valuable where you live, the opportunity to acquire a property like this in a desert region might actually be an albatross. In extremely hot regions, taller houses can be exponentially more expensive due to air conditioning, and in the end, actually worth less. Without local knowledge, you could think you're getting a great deal until you realize the property is completely illiquid and unsellable. Data is very important.

Twenty years ago, we entered our least successful deal in Chennai. We bought a property in an urban location using 100 percent debt, and because we had to put down a guarantee, we didn't make any money on the development. We developed 120 apartments, and we had to use our equity and other projects just to finance this one. We were over-leveraged, and when you're leveraged too high, the entire profit can get expunged very quickly.

Different people believe in different leverage percentages, but what I can tell you is that when you're over-leveraged—anything above 80 percent loan-to-cost or loan-to-value—if *anything* goes wrong, you will run into trouble. There is a zero margin for error and that is not realistic.

When analyzing real estate, I look for three key elements. My family is mainly in the residential business, so we focus on location, price, and momentum of sales. The classic cliché of "location, location, location" has turned out to be true in our case in India. Once we find the correct location on a main avenue with good ingress/egress, one near public transportation and other services, we then study the market and analyze the demand to determine if the price we can sell the units at makes sense in this market. Once we begin selling units in a new building, we start to build up momentum that we can use to our advantage.

No matter how large your company, you still need to consult external market research. We seek data on the current prices people are paying in the region and how fast purchases are occurring. If we like what the data we buy says, we then launch our own internal study—we don't just rely on external information. Use a combination of external and internal research and data to gain the clearest and most comprehensive perspective possible. No matter what property type you are looking at, or where in the world you are; I always recommend you do this.

Starting Over

If I were just starting out today, I would be doing the exact same thing. I have a passion for residential real estate and hotels. Hotels are my favorite type of project to build and maintain. In the past, I experimented with other types of real estate. I developed some office buildings, and eventually we sold them off to a strategic fund because we believe real estate is a local business, and we like to focus on the areas that we understand.

India is unique in that multifamily homes don't make sense because the interest rates are 10 to 12 percent of the cost. While duplexes and quadplexes might be amazing in America, for our market, it's hard to build them profitably, especially when you're just starting out.

Don't forget the value of diversifying your income streams. Prepare yourself for real estate markets to grow and shrink, and for shifts in the market that don't come directly from real estate cycles. If the market gets crowded or a lot of other companies come to compete with you in one area of your business, having other areas will keep you strong. You will avoid forcing yourself to make a deal you would normally not make or accept a price you normally wouldn't take.

Market Shocks

I'm a big believer in opening up multiple revenue streams so you can focus on whichever one is the right stream at any given time. Before entering a new market, look for the greatest demand and supply imbalance. For example, in India at the moment, there are more people than homes. There is a significant home deficit, and people will always need a place to live.

When it comes to financing, at a certain point you'll have to take on debt or leverage to scale up your company or side business. You want to protect yourself as much as possible and not take on too much debt. I like to have more equity than debt and maintain a 60:40 percent equity-to-debt ratio for my projects. I believe that this ratio puts you in a strong position to survive economic downturns, surprises, and crises that may arise.

No matter how lucrative the upside, never close a deal without looking at the property in person. Things that look amazing on paper might not be that great when you see them in their real context. You might find that within an apartment building you can purchase some really great units at below replacement cost. Nonetheless, it turns out that there are 50 other units for sale in the same complex. I've seen projects where more than 60 percent of the units have been on sale for multiple years, and they just don't get absorbed for different reasons: The apartments might be too big for the local market surrounding the project. The mix of rooms is incorrect. The amenities are not there. People don't like the design or quality of the building. Or other factors may come into play.

Get ready for deals that underperform. Do your best to minimize the downside and always rely on your common sense. Get as much data as you can so that when you enter a deal, you have as much data as possible. The more you know before you go into a deal, the more likely it is to end up profitable.

There's currently a big real estate shift in India that I don't think is a good idea. It's called "land banking," and this is where developers take on debt to purchase land and keep buying more, putting out more guarantees and putting themselves in a highly levered position. They're unbelievably vulnerable to an imminent market shock.

Technology

I believe that technology is going to affect every real estate market. Within the retail industry there has been massive disruption due to Amazon and other technological innovations that have pushed a growing number of consumers to mobile purchases and e-commerce. In the office sector, WeWork and other workspace companies are transforming the way we function in and carry out our jobs. Traditionally, office environments have been places where employees go to work Monday through Friday from roughly 9 to 5. This is now changing.

Car riding service and driverless cars will have an impact on all real estate segments in different levels. Within the hotel space, we have seen that Airbnb and other similar companies have affected the lower and middle end of the market. In Appaswamy we focus on the top of the market—the luxury and five-star segment—and within this arena of the market, technology is still not affecting but rather complementing.

The top echelon of the market likes the luxury hotel experience, and we are making sure we upgrade our hotel rooms with smart technology to stay ahead of the competition. At the moment, we are building a high-end residential building in Chennai, one of India's largest cities. It's going to be a smart tower where you can control the entire apartment from an iPad. It will also have several green and environmentally friendly components, something we believe are also very important to include in your projects these days.

From a sales angle, it's critical to use technology because the internet and social media play an essential role today when it comes to selling and leasing properties.

My Philosophy

When it comes to the balance between mindset and technical skills, I believe that mindset is far more important. You're going to spend a lot of time with yourself, and all that time when you're alone, you have to believe in yourself and in your projects.

In terms of mentors, as I come from a family business, my father and my grandfather both inspired, educated, and trained me. In addition to them, I look up to Stephen Ross from Related Companies in the United States and Simon Chung in Singapore. These are two extraordinary real estate investors who have taught me so much.

My favorite book is *The Art of the Deal* by Donald Trump. I read it when I was a kid, and it is still one of my favorite readings.

If all I could leave my children were three real estate recommendations, these would be it:

1. Be alert to seize an opportunity.
2. Be patient and wait for the right opportunity.
3. Be balanced while dealing with challenges.

Key Principles

- Stick to a very small sector within real estate in terms of segments and geography. You must have a clear focus and vision for your real estate business.

- The real estate industry is very small; all the players in the local market know each other. Take care of your name and your reputation above all else.

- When you're developing in a place that you don't know as well, big surprises will come your way. Anticipate them as best you can.

- When you take on too much leverage your profits can get wiped out very quickly, and you can sometimes lose all of your equity. Be careful with taking on too much debt.

- The famous adage in real estate about "location, location, location" turns out to be true. Be disciplined about location.

- Try to diversify your income streams in real estate. Prepare yourself for real estate markets to grow and shrink and for shifts in the market that don't come directly from real estate cycles.

- Find niches and areas within real estate where supply and demand imbalances exist.

- Be prepared for the shifts in technology; every single segment in real estate is being or will be affected in different ways by technology.

- Finding a good mentor will help you reach your goals faster and make fewer mistakes along the way.

Exercise

Your reputation is the most important asset you have in the world of real estate, more important than money. If you lose your money but maintain your good name, you will eventually recover your money with hunger driving you. But if your reputation gets tarnished and you lose your good name, it will be very hard for you to keep making money. The real estate market is small and even if you are not managing other people's money, you still need to have relationships with potential sellers, partners, banks, brokers, and consultants, among others, and therefore it is vital that you always follow the law and do what is right.

The following is an example intended to make you think about your own values and ethics. Imagine you have entered a joint venture with a long-time friend of yours who is a trustworthy and prominent developer in Eastern Europe.

You have partnered to develop three business-class hotels in a made-up emerging country called Jaber. You have acquired the three properties, well-situated empty land lots, with the money of institutional investors from the United Kingdom. You have a fiduciary duty to them. You are now in the conceptualization phase, advancing with design and architecture works and marketing your project with the local government—to obtain permits and licenses—and explaining to them that your new hotels will create hundreds of new jobs, increase taxes, improve the beauty of the city, and more. The mayor who oversees the development in that city gets back to you saying he would love for you to develop the project and will give you all the necessary permits and licenses; however, he needs to receive a payment from you—as he does from all other developers in the area—for his own personal benefit. Otherwise he will be unable to help you with this process and your project will likely suffer a long delay. What do you do? Does the reward justify the risk? Will this affect your reputation?

Chapter 10

Joseph Sitt
Thor Equities
New York, New York, USA

Photo credit: Zev Starr-Tambor

Learn to understand customers and what they want

Perhaps best known as the King of high streets, Joe Sitt has been a visionary in the real estate and retail industries. For years, many proclaimed that high streets are in a decline and no longer have an allure to them, Joe however, has had a different opinion. He believes that that high streets around the world will continue to be an important place where fun and innovative, consumer focused businesses will grow and thrive. High streets, such as the Champs Elysees in Paris and Bond Street in London, have been around blossoming since the late 1700s. That means these streets have endured the world's greatest wars, famines, plagues, depressions, civil clashes, global recessions, and more. And Joe believes they will endure e-commerce, social commerce, virtual reality, 3-D printing, and other future technologies. Why? Because these avenues have positioned themselves as cultural landmarks, historic hearts of their cities where elegance and beautiful design meet fun social gatherings. Like the Champs-Élysées and Bond Street, there are a myriad of other beautiful high streets all around the world's major cities. 5th Avenue in New York, La Rambla in Barcelona, and Via Spiga in Milan are just a few others. Thor Equities, the real estate company Joe Sitt founded while in college, owns properties in several of these high streets—and others—around the world.

In His Own Words

Since I was a kid I always had a passion for real estate. I grew up in New York City, which is so rich in diversity and culture. I enjoyed walking through the five boroughs of New York and learning about the different cultures and people. That fit well with my passion for buildings, retail, design, and deal making. From an early age I appreciated the demanding nature of ground-up development, of the financial engineering required in real estate, and of the challenges with raising capital.

I have always loved traveling to different cities and countries and seeing wonderful people living and working and shopping within well-designed spaces. Today, I am blessed to be a macro investor and developer in real estate all around the world, and therefore I am a global tourist.

Starting Out

When I was 19 years old, while I was studying at New York University, I cherished walking through the different parts of the city. I would mostly walk through Manhattan, Brooklyn, Queens, and the Bronx. I knew most of the streets and areas by heart. There was a retail property in the Bronx that I ended up sourcing through a personal relationship. At the time there was a very bad recession in real estate in the United States. I knew this was a good property because it was near public transportation, there was a lot of density surrounding the property, and I had a tenant—Rainbow Shoes—interested in the location. I realized I needed equity, which I did not have, to buy the property. Therefore, what I did was sign a leasing agreement with this credit-worthy tenant *before* buying the property, and then I was able to get a financing institution to put up the debt because of the signed lease. The bank required a little equity up front. I had invited a builder I knew to join me in the deal; he put up the required equity and in exchange became be my partner in the deal. I was able to carry out the transaction by only putting in my "sweat equity". We all did really well on that first transaction.

As time went on, I did other deals in the Bronx and I learned about all kinds of trends in the boroughs. Through these deals I learned about inner-city retail customer tastes and needs. I noticed there was an opportunity in women's clothing in plus sizes in urban areas, and I founded an apparel brand called Ashley Stewart. I grew the company to over 420 stores. Eventually I decided it was time to sell. I enjoyed being a retailer, but I wanted to return to real estate, which had always been my passion.

Valuable Lessons from the Stock Market

My worst investment was an equity play in the stock market. I invested in a manufacturing company, an area where I had no expertise, and there were several good lessons for me as a result.

The first was to focus on my strengths. The real estate market is what I knew best, and manufacturing was not an area of expertise for me.

The second important lesson is that while it is always important to have a diversified portfolio in terms of assets, currencies and geographies, you have to be cognizant that as a passive investor, you have no control over the outcome of an investment.

The third important lesson learned is that when you make any type of investment in a business or company that you do not control, you should study the senior management or the person in charge. Who is leading the business? What is his or her track record doing this? Who else is on the senior management team with them? At the end, this senior management will be the most important thing driving the business or company; so know that you are ultimately making an investment in them.

Approaching Real Estate Deals

When acquiring real estate properties there are so many things to consider, certainly too many to name in this conversation. But let me share several things we do at Thor.

In real estate, deals are only available for a finite period—especially the very good ones—so it is important to move fast.

It is also important to find out as much as you as can about the seller. Some relevant questions to consider are: Why do they want to sell the property? What is their full-time job and how sophisticated are they in real estate? Do we know the lowest selling price they would accept? As a note, I always recommend establishing rapport with the seller. Real estate is a business of relationships; the better your relationships with other market players, the more success you should have.

As we look at the specific opportunity, what are the macro variables? Do we feel comfortable with the current environment in terms of interest rates, inflation projections, unemployment, and so forth? If we are looking at emerging markets, do we feel comfortable with the foreign exchange risk? What are the supply and demand dynamics of that specific market?

Other things to consider are more local to the market, such as the growth of the fixed population in that city or district. What is the average age of the population? Who among them could be my final users? Are they mainly Millennials? If so, what technologies do they use that could influence the project? Is the floating population (leisure or business tourism) growing? What are the legal and tax frameworks in this market like? What is the political situation in this specific city or country?

Interestingly, if you study great businessmen in history such as Benjamin Franklin, Walt Disney, Steve Jobs, and today Jeff Bezos, you will learn that they had great vision. They always tried to predict trends decades ahead of their time. As you make any type of real estate investment in property, ask yourself where you think this investment will be in 10 to 20 years. I always ask myself what the neighborhood will be like 20 years from now. Don't be overly focused on what the market looks like today; look at it with a long-term vision because real estate is a long-term investment. It might not be for you, but it could be for the buyer you sell it to.

In terms of financial analysis, I am a big believer that going in, cap rates are only one way to look at properties. It is much more relevant to analyze what you think the cap rate could be in two to five years with the correct strategy and execution. I am not a majority core investor; historically at Thor, we add value to our properties by redesigning and re-tenanting buildings and sometimes developing from the ground up. Besides yield (cap rate) we also focus on the equity multiple and internal rate of return over given hold periods.

I also look at how much financing I will be able to obtain from a financial institution? What are the terms of the loan? While on the subject of financing, a note on debt: It is important not to overleverage your investment. It is always very tempting to take on more debt if a financial institution is willing to lend you the money, but proceed with caution. When you are in the good parts of the cycle, leverage will help you do better. But when you are in the bottom of the cycle leverage can wipe you out of your investment. If you were buying properties in United States I would say that as a maximum you take 70 percent loan to value. If you are in an emerging market, 55 percent is probably something that makes more sense. Needless to say, the stability of the asset (lease term, tenancy, etc.) greatly impacts this decision.

Opportunities

In general, an important rule to follow is to try and focus on making deals in areas where most people are not, and investing in times when most people are not. No matter what the situation is, you always need to use solid, fundamental analysis as part of your decision-making process. But if you can do this and buy properties when there is a clear market supply and demand imbalance, then even better.

If you are a risk-taking entrepreneurial investor, I suggest you start looking at Africa. It has a young and growing population.

Some 200 million Africans are between 15 and 24, and it is the fastest growing continent on the planet in terms of people, and over the next 30 years the population will grow by one billion. The economies are getting stronger and more diverse and the middle class is growing.

Favorite Deal

I am blessed to have made hundreds of real estate transactions in my life, and fortunately so many interesting investments in all types of sectors and geographies. Everything we do at Thor has a lot of history; we like investing in properties that have cultural meaning and in those that society already thinks of as important buildings and landmarks.

One such property is Burlington Arcade in London. It has a special meaning to me because we acquired and restored the oldest retail shopping center in the Western world, situated in one of the most prominent locations in downtown London—right behind Bond Street, one of the world's preeminent high streets. The deal was very profitable for our investors. I believe the property will remain a treasured London destination for generations to come.

Common Mistakes and Mindsets

The biggest mistakes I have seen other real estate players make are overleveraging, doing business with untrustworthy individuals, and undervaluing their brand name.

In real estate you can usually afford to make some mistakes—especially when you are in good locations—and survive the downturns. However, if you overleverage your investment and you go through a downturn, that is one mistake that will be very hard to come back from.

Another mistake that players make is they enter a market without knowing who they are doing business with. I always tell my team: a good deal with a bad partner is a bad deal. You should always be prepared for real estate to be a long-term investment, so you want to work with partners you can trust.

The third mistake I have seen others make is not understanding the importance of their reputation. How honest you are with partners, investors, institutions, final users and other players is essential. You need to be honorable and to keep your word; in doing so, your brand will allow you to get investors, financing, tenants, buyers, and more. Nothing is more important than your brand.

Some of the things I tell my children who are now entering the real estate business is to work very hard. Take care of their reputation above everything else. Love what they do because if they love what they do then success and money will follow.

I have also talked to them about the importance of psychology. Having a powerful mindset is not only true in real estate, it's true in every other business arena and is essential. Your mindset, your determination, your hunger, and your drive are all correlated.

Technical skills are obviously great to have, and numbers are very important in real estate, but having a powerful mindset comes before that. If you believe in yourself, you will find a way to succeed. There is a story from Hernan Cortes about mindset that I think has some important lessons.

In 1519, he led a large expedition consisting of over 600 Spaniards to Veracruz, Mexico. Upon his arrival, Cortes ordered his men to burn the ships. He wanted to send a very clear message: There was no turning back. We either accomplish our goal of finding great treasure, or we die trying. Within two years Cortes and his men conquered the Aztec empire. This strategy was implemented by Cortes to expunge any notion of failure from the minds of his soldiers. They were forced to adopt a mindset of profound belief that they would succeed.

Mentorship

Being an entrepreneur is exciting as you start a new company and try to take on the world. But in reality, there are many unforeseen and unexpected things that will come up along the way. For example, in real estate you can suddenly be dealing with some type of political turmoil, natural disaster, geopolitical war, a new disrupting technology, local market disturbances, or numerous other issues. Most of the time, these are factors that you will not expect or be able to control; but there are always steps you can to take to protect your business and your projects from these types of challenges.

If you are young it is likely that you will not have had the experience to deal with these adversities, and so it´s good to have someone with life and business experience to guide you through many of these challenges and shorten your learning curve. It is also good to have a mentor who can pass on other important lessons.

I've had a few different mentors over the years and learned numerous valuable lessons from each one of them. My father was my greatest mentor. From a very young age he taught me the valuable lessons of being extremely hard working and being very honest. Those two values are deeply ingrained in me, and this is something that I have endeavored to pass on to the people closest to me. My dad used to say that when it comes to integrity, there is no gray, there is only back and white.

My father also taught me to dream big. I learned from him that it is important to dare to dream; if you are hungry you will find the way to make your dreams happen.

Technology in Real Estate

Technology is disrupting every segment and market in real estate. As a general rule, it is lowering the amount of space that people need. In retail we have obviously seen the effects of online shopping; in the office we are seeing more and more people work from home; in the hotel sector we are seeing Airbnb and similar firms having an impact; in the residential sector, co-living and smart homes are making a big impact.

Car sharing services have exploded all around the world, and we are a few years away from driverless cars in the United States. Now 3-D printing is a reality, and it's just a matter of time until we see how this affects construction and costs. Real estate fintech start-ups (those that use technology to automate and improve financial services) are now becoming players in the market. Robotics and cognitive automation are also an up and coming technology that can affect real estate in the coming years. Software, apps, and technologies that we currently don't even know about will have effects on the industry. Anyone in real estate needs to be prepared for these coming changes.

Routines

I read a lot about things that have nothing to do with real estate. I read newspapers from all around the world because I do business all around the world. I read about science and new inventions. I read art-related magazines and history books. I read about technology and other fields that I like. I apply a lot from what I read to my business.

I also read the traditional papers like the *New York Times* and the *Wall Street Journal*, as well as magazines like the *Economist* and the *New Yorker*.

Two of my favorite books are *Tuesdays with Morrie* by Mitch Albom and *The Ultimate Gift* by Jim Stovall. I love both these books because they put perspective on what's important in life.

Other parts of my morning routine are that I exercise several days a week and I pray every day.

Final Thoughts

I am a believer that if you have integrity nothing else matters. It's the most important asset you can have in business.

The only money you will take to the afterlife is the money you gave back to charity and good causes during your time on earth.

I think a fulfilled life comes from a balance of two perspectives: I looked at a psychological study once conducted with 98 elderly people who were in their hospital beds. When they were asked about their biggest regrets in life, they did not mention anything that they did, but they regretted many of the things they never had the courage to do. So I believe it's best to be grateful for what we were given and live life with no regrets.

As a wise man once told me, "Happiness is not getting what you want, happiness is wanting what you already have." I love this quote. Many of us go through life trying to achieve so much, and while that might be great, true happiness is found when we are grateful for what we have.

Key Takeaways

- It is important to walk the neighborhoods and streets in areas where you are considering investing to understand customer tastes and preferences.
- You can carry out deals by putting in very little or no equity, but to do so requires creativity and having people who trust you.

- Analyzing any investment opportunity from both a quantitative and qualitative way is essential to avoid making many mistakes.

- There are numerous traits that are important to possess as you seek success in real estate, but a powerful mindset is the most important one.

- Above all else make sure to keep your integrity and good name. It is your most valuable asset.

Exercise

For the following week after you finish reading this book, do something every day to strengthen your mindset. The great minds, like the one that Joseph Sitt has, envision a world where anything is possible. They are intellectually curious. Here are some things you could do: listen to an inspiring podcast, meet with a mentor you already have and explore new topics in the conversation, read a book that will expand your level of thinking, meditate to explore a new kind awareness, and join a mastermind group of real estate professionals who will lift you higher and who are willing to share their thoughts and expertise.

Chapter 11

Carlos Betancourt

Bresco
Sao Paulo, Brazil

Patience is the ultimate virtue

L eonardo Davinci, one of the great minds in human history, said that "simplicity is the ultimate sophistication." As
I spoke to Carlos Betancourt it became evident to me that
one of his life mantras is to keep things simple, a way of living that
many of the world's greatest follow. Understanding the laws of supply
and demand, comprehending the different cycles, and realizing that

liquidity equals value, are all fundamental truths in real estate. These offer a point of view through which Carlos sees potential investment opportunities and ways to mitigate some risks. If you are a seeker of information, and a serious observer that knows how to separate the noise from the meaningful, it's all there to be seized and learned.

Simplicity is not easy to achieve. Distilling complex ideas into coherent and simple thoughts can be hard work and take time. Carlos is a champion at doing this. As we conversed, two professional advantages became clear about having this ability. First, is that it allows you to focus on being good at what you do. Second, it allows to communicate in a better way with your employees, investors, suppliers, final users, etc. about what you are trying to do.

In His Own Words

The real estate business is embedded within my DNA, and I knew from an early age that it was my destiny. My family has been in the real estate game for generations.

My father was a major influence in my life. He passed away three years ago, and not a day goes by that I don't miss him. He was born in Cuba when it was still a free country. Shortly after his marriage to my mother, Castro took over the country and turned it into a dictatorship.

My father's family was not in the real estate business, however. They were in the business of ready-mixed concrete. My father decided to leave while freedom was still a possibility. Working as a manager in Cuba, he took his knowledge to Brazil to see if he could make a better life for him and my mother and their future family.

At the time, the ready-mixed concrete business did not exist in Brazil, and he wanted to expand there. My father didn't speak a word of Portuguese, but an uncle lent him enough money to get started. With just three trucks, he built the foundation of a new business in a foreign country.

My father brought a new industry to Brazil and had the advantage of being the first one in a new construction market. Soon, he was one of the biggest builders in the region, with several hundred trucks across Brazil and Uruguay. My brother and I grew up in that business, and we played at the plant when we were younger.

The leap from construction to real estate is not a very big one. I simply built on my father's existing connections.

Although the sands of time can sometimes make it hard to remember some of my deals, I can still remember where and when it all began. In pursuit of a first real estate deal, I was determined to convince my family about a certain location where there were some residential houses. I discovered that the government had recently changed the zoning in this area to increase floor-to-area ratio (FAR) and allow vertical construction. I started thinking big, and I saw a lot of value there.

This was a very ambitious first project; to acquire a large piece of land, we would have to buy 12 homes. Fortunately, I was able to assemble the entire block and acquire all the sites.

That deal taught me one of the most important lessons in real estate: You must have a great deal of patience because things change all the time. One guy would sell his house one month, and the next month another guy would change his mind about selling.

In the end, we put the land together and built 12 office towers. While we took on a lot of risk, it turned out to be a massive success. It took a longer time than expected but it was worth the effort and patience.

My Favorite Deal

My favorite deal is a piece of land that we bought about eight years ago right next to the most important cargo airport in Brazil, called Viracopos International. According to the Department of Civil

Aviation, this is the best airport in the country. *Air Cargo World* considers it one of the best-run airports in the world. It's one hour from the center of Sao Paulo, Brazil.

I bought some land that's right next to the airport. It's not residential, but I used to joke that it was ocean-front. It's one of the best locations in Brazil because it's next to the trains, the airport, and the best highways. It's an amazing location, but it wasn't easy.

Getting the right documentation was a battle. Even as we were acquiring the land, we were still dealing with government delays and red tape.

We had to buy the land, and for the majority of the payments, we had to make the payment contingent on getting the right paperwork. It took two years. The land was designed to be mixed-use, and in the city of Campinas the process was very bureaucratic.

After buying the land, it took another four years to acquire the building on the site. In the end, the struggle was worth it.

I built a miniature city with offices, hotels, shops, a park with a running track, and a huge fitness center. Security was one of my primary concerns, and we were able to build an entire community where people can live securely and happy. There are certain dangers to living and being successful in Brazil, and we built a safe community that limits those dangers.

Upon completion of the project, I was also able to dedicate a plaza to my dad, making this project especially important to me.

Hard Lessons

There are lessons to be learned in both humility and real estate from my least successful deal.

There's a city called Manaus in the state of Amazon, north of Brazil. We won an intense bidding process to build a warehouse there, and in the process we used one of the top three law firms in the country to perform our due diligence.

We bought the land, created the design, and began construction. As the trucks began to roll in, some guys came to the lot saying they owned the land and asking what we were doing on their property.

It turned out that the person who sold us the land initially had used fake documents. He had never owned the land. I was mystified. I couldn't believe it. The notary was in on the scam. Fortunately, I had obtained title insurance to protect my downside.

We began speaking with other players in the area, and we discovered that there were many similar cases. This was a lesson that showed how local the business real estate development really is. Even when you are in your own country, each state and city has its own rules and ways. Certain regions can be completely different, and in this case lawless.

In the south of Brazil, there is law and structure. But in the north, it's the Wild West. The danger of moving into new regions exists everywhere. If you are in real estate, each time you move into a new region, you have to adhere to market data and local experts. If you start to think that the rules are the same just because you're in the "same country," you will very likely make mistakes that could cause you huge losses. This deal was a five-hour flight from where I'd previously done business.

Exercise caution. If you are entering a new market, it makes sense to partner with a good trustworthy local player.

When starting out in real estate it's best to choose a single region and focus on mastering the business there. Go as deep as possible with your knowledge and expertise. Don't try to build warehouses across your entire country or single-family homes in a dozen different cities. Focus on a region and focus on a specific segment.

Risky Business

When I'm looking for a property, whether I'm going to build, buy some land, or convert houses into office buildings, the first things I try to analyze are the three cycles (see Figure 11.1).

In the places where I'm investing I study the economic cycle, the political cycle (especially in Brazil), and the real estate cycle. Are interest rates going up or down? Are the politicians going to increase or decrease regulation? Is there a game-changing bill working its way through the local government? Are tax laws changing? Has the new president promised to make some changes to the real estate landscape? Are there new large players in the market? Are banks lending developers and buyers?

Real estate goes through cycles where, at times, there might be more buyers than there is supply. The reverse may be true. It changes relatively quickly. I look at all three main cycles to determine if I should be investing and, if so, in what properties and in what neighborhoods.

Everyone has a personal perspective on when it's time to be risky and when it's time to be conservative. Maybe I'm a bit contrarian, but when the market is tight, players are not very active, and people are building speculatively, I try to jump in with my money. That's my macro analysis.

Whenever I see something I'm interested in, I go to the location. I walk the property, the site, the neighborhood, and the city. Understand the fundamentals.

It's very important to determine the value and the quality of the location. If I like the location, and it passes my first test, I look at the economics of the deal. Does it make sense financially? Is it well leveraged in a reasonable way?

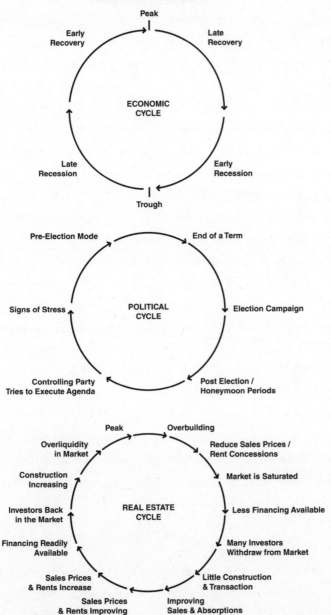

Figure 11.1 Three main cycles—economic, political, and real estate.

I invest in properties around the world, so I like to invest in a property that appeals to multiple tenants. If it appeals to just one type of person or a single industry, I get a little concerned.

If I were to go all the way back to my late teens or early 20s, and I was just getting into real estate without the good fortune to follow my father's successful footsteps, I would have started with residential real estate. At the end of the day, people will always need a place to live. Especially in Brazil, where there's so much need for housing, and there's so much that we can provide.

Logistics are very important. Technology won't eliminate the need for logistics. Disruption won't happen as much in this segment and it might actually increase the need for logistics.

I also like buying residential within mixed-use properties where you can create a sense of community because, especially in Brazil, we have so many issues with transportation and security. People want to live, shop, and work in the same place, so these are the three main factors for me.

I'm not a fan of investing in commercial properties such as retail and hotels. I have some holdings there, but that's not the core of my business.

If you're looking at long-term real estate investments, and are willing to take emerging market risk, there are some very interesting things happening in India, China, Brazil, and South Africa.

Leverage

There are different ways to use leverage. If you're investing for your own personal use, it's good to use some leverage as long as you're disciplined. If you don't have leverage, its much more difficult to buy the property because real estate is capital-intensive. You have to know the risks and you need to be sure you will have the capacity to pay that loan.

If you're an investor, be very careful with how much money you borrow from the bank. At my firm, Bracor, we try to stay between 45 and 60 percent loan-to-value ratio. We ask ourselves very carefully if the deal makes sense.

When we invested in real estate in Japan, the banks there lent us money at a rate of just 1 percent a year. It was like free money, and we knew we could increase our leverage significantly. In Brazil, on the other hand, there were times when the banks charged us crippling double-digit interest rates for access to their leverage. They asked for too much money, and we simply couldn't afford to do the deal. We had to let those deals float away because the risk was too high.

At Bracor, our approach is more conservative. We like to use self-amortizing loans where the lease agreements are tied to the leverage we take. No matter what tools your employ to minimize your exposure to leverage, don't get lost in the emotion and overleverage your property or portfolio.

Many people first entering the real estate market are still working 9 to 5 jobs. It's easy for them to mistake a real estate deal for a financial transaction, but real estate is not liquid in the way true financial assets are. When investing in stocks and mutual funds, it's quite easy to turn them back into cash. Real estate isn't like that. You can't turn a property into cash unless you have a buyer.

Even extremely wealthy and experienced investors can make this mistake when entering the world of real estate. They come in and think that flipping real estate is like buying and selling a stock, but that's a big mistake.

The asset is a property, and as a property, there are maintenance fees, vacancies, and real estate taxes. Keep all that in mind. If you own a stock in a company, it's not going to go down in value if there's a kidnapping in the neighborhood or if a water pipe bursts in the winter and floods the house.

A property is very different from traditional financial assets. As you invest, pay attention to where you are in the three cycles. Don't jump in when things are expensive just because you saw a positive newsfeed.

In real estate, patience is the ultimate virtue; real estate is not a liquid asset. As you invest and look at your first properties, always think about quality. If you're just looking for a fast rate of return, you will probably be disappointed. By quality, I mean a good location within a market that has demand and where the asset has quality construction.

How is the property useful for the actual needs of our society? Do you need to make capital expenditures to improve or maintain the property? How does the property appeal to people? What type of infrastructure surrounds the property or project? Is there going to be a new highway or new transportation built near there soon? Is there a chance something negative can be built there? What's happening in the market? Are all the permits in good standing? How far is a gym, a tarbucks and public transportation?

These questions are just the beginning of the due diligence process.

Obviously, I recommend that you make sure the person you're dealing with actually owns the property. Hopefully, my mistake will prevent you from having to deal with a similar situation.

Operating from a place of need is very dangerous. It leaves you vulnerable to poor and dangerous decision-making.

My team quotes me almost on a daily basis because I always try to be in a position where I approach a deal as a wish or a desire, not as a need. Many players feel like they *need* to buy or they *need* to sell to reach the next level of lifestyle or simply because of their pride. When that happens, it normally translates into a bad deal.

If you want to buy or sell something that you need, you'll rarely end up with a good deal. This is where emotion enters the equation.

We don't want to enter that "auction excitement," We want to be driven by the analytical, logical part of our minds, not the emotional part of our hearts.

By approaching a deal as a wish rather than a need, I believe you become less emotional and more rational.

Technology

Interestingly, technology is really changing the game. Logistics are not getting replaced, but now we have Airbnb competing with hotels. There are apps like LiquidSpace in the office sector, and Amazon is significantly impacting the retail space on a global level.

In the last couple of years, I've tried to be very connected with how the disruption of technology is affecting the real estate market. I'm constantly trying to learn from technology companies.

I go to the Silicon Valley for meetings to speak with the senior managers at Uber, Airbnb, Google, and several other tech companies. Technology is a big issue, and it's a reality.

I think that autonomous vehicles will have a major effect on all industries, and they will change the way we design shopping centers and property in general—even in small areas, like where we park.

My main worry is that we're going to move into a more data-driven industry. One of the companies I've invested in is already doing this and using a lot of data to help in their decision-making process.

I'm concerned with where the different technological tools intersect with consumer demands. There are so many new tools for consumer "needs," and there's so much data, that it can become overwhelming.

The average person thinks real estate is just about knowledge—just about hitting the books and learning about cap rates, and then you can start making a lot of money. But the truth is, success in this world is heavily driven by emotional temperament. I'm often sur-rounded by extremely smart people from very prestigious schools and top companies—and honestly, they have higher IQs than I do. They have fancy computers and software, but they don't think about the big picture because they're too focused on the math, the numbers, and the little details.

When you have that mindset, you get tunnel vision, and you only think about one piece of that big picture.

Leadership Skills

Leadership skills develop in a continuing a process. If you aren't improving them, they are atrophying. Try to find ways to inspire and motivate others. Leadership in real estate isn't just about doing the math and snatching a profit. Sometimes, you need to create a type of empathy and inspire the person on the other side of the deal or the person on your own team. We're in a business where we can dramat-ically affect the destiny of many people.

In real estate, we're buying and selling homes where people live or buildings where people work. The last thing I want to do is take away someone's livelihood or home. I always think, "Am I making this place better?" My goal when entering a deal is, of course, to make a profit, but not at the cost of my own sense of morality or identity. I'm not out to crush my final users. I want to add value to all of them and the community.

You can make a lot of money in the real estate world without ever doing something that you later regret—without building ene-mies or making people feel like you took advantage of them in their moment of need.

You never know when you might have your own moment of need. Some of the biggest real estate companies in the world have been smashed during recessions. Whether or not you believe in karma, the energy you put out into the world comes back many times over.

That deal in which you took advantage of one person 10 years ago might haunt you in the future, the next time a recession hits the market. You'll be the one in the vulnerable position, and someone else could do the same thing to you, only at 10 or 100 times the scale.

As a leader, it's important to understand the elements of psychology. I try to inject as much self-belief into my team as possible. I want the people who do deals with me to walk away feeling great. I try to predict possible problems five years into the future.

While your personality drives your ability to lead, continuing to learn is also critical. No matter how successful you become, there is always more you can learn. I've seen this in my partnership with Sam Zell. He's very objective and literal. Whenever I use a metaphor or a symbol, it goes right over his head, but he has an incredible sense of psychology. He's a tremendous winner—success isn't just for one personality type.

My father and Sam have been the prime mentors in my life. My father taught me about ethics, perseverance, and passion. And in my partnership with Sam, for such a long time, I have been inspired by his vision, objectivity, and unbelievable business skills.

Maintaining your fitness and health is also important. Real estate is about patience in a long-term game. The better your health is, the more time you have with which to operate. I encourage you not to sacrifice your health to build your business. You'll only regret it as you shorten your life.

I have a passion for the sport of rowing. I've been an athlete for more than 40 years. I started in my teens, and I was a member of the junior national team in Brazil. When you're rowing, you have to get up at 5:30 in the morning every day to practice. It really impacted my schedule. I've even run 15 different marathons. For more than 20 years, I've competed in triathlons regularly, and I still compete.

I exercise seven days a week. I know people will tell you to take days off, but there's something in my DNA, and I feel lazy when I skip an exercise day. Exercise helps me in everything else that I do. I also enjoy surfing and boxing. I go to the Maldives a couple of times a year just to surf with my daughters.

I've been experimenting with meditation for the past year. I always thought I'd be the last guy to try that out, but I see a lot of value in it now. I also have a little bit of a musical streak; I play percussion.

I try to help the kids in the slums in Sao Paulo, and the two biggest passions for disadvantaged children there are soccer and percussion. It's the two best ways to help them escape the favelas of Brazil.

We've helped hundreds of kids throughout the years. I didn't start the charity group, but I got in early when there were just 15 or 20 kids. We've opened concerts for people like Madonna, John Mayer, Wynton Marsalis, and many other amazing artists.

We performed a show for a board of trustees, and someone said, "Imagine if these kids could play halftime at a football game." And I said, "Let's make it happen."

A month later, we got a letter from the University of Notre Dame. Fifty kids from the favelas, one of the toughest places in the world to grow up, were invited to go to South Bend, Indiana, to perform in a game between Notre Dame and Stanford.

They asked me to be a trustee, and I'd only been there for four years.

My Philosophy

You have to try to educate yourself as much as possible. When mu parents left Cuba, they didn't have a dollar to their names. I learned that you could be stripped of everything, but all your experience and education would be with you for the rest of your life. You'll be able to use knowledge for the good of humankind, for your family, for your community, and to pass on to your children.

You must try to balance your life. It's not just about business or just about having fun; it's about so many other things. As much as I'm honored to be called a Real Estate Titan and to be interviewed for this book, I would hesitate to give myself a nickname like that. I would hesitate to say that my life is perfect. I still haven't achieved the perfect balance. I haven't completed my education. My story isn't over.

I'm not a monument on top of a mountain. I'm just someone who's farther along than others, a little bit closer to the peak. But I'm still trying to find my perfect balance.

It's okay if you don't get it right. The journey is just as important as the destination.

Life is short. Do everything you can to enjoy every minute of your life. Build a business around things that you like. Follow your passion and use that to find the right path to reap your profits. Real estate can be an amazing and fun venture.

Key Principles

- You must have the ability to plan long-term and realize that there is always a downturn. People's memories are usually shorter than the cycles.
- Know that the real estate development business is a cyclical one, and that each state and city has different local elements and laws that you need to learn about.
- When starting out in real estate it's best to choose a single region and focus on mastering the business there. Go as deep as possible with your knowledge and expertise.
- There are three important cycles you should be aware of, the economic, political and real estate cycles. Before

making an investment, you should always analyze where you
are in all three.

- In real estate it's best to be a contrarian. When the market
  is tight, players are not very active, banks are barely lending
  money to investors, and people are building speculatively, it
  should be a good time to buy.

- As you look to invest in your first properties, always think
  about quality. If you're just looking for a quick return, you
  will likely be disappointed. By quality, I mean a good location within a market that has solid demand and where the
  asset has quality construction.

- Patience, patience, and more patience. Real estate is a long-
  term game; don't think of it as a short-term investment.

- When you invest in real estate always try to leave emotion
  out. You want to be driven by the numbers and logic, not by
  emotion or ego.

- You can be stripped of your money and assets but no one
  can ever take away your brain or your knowledge. Feed your
  mind everyday and use it for the good of humankind.

Exercise

Carlos talks about three main cycles that he analyzes—
economic, political, and real estate—to determine if he should
be investing and, if so, in what properties and in what neighborhoods. Whenever you are looking to make an investment in
real estate, draw out these three cycles and try as best you can
to determine where you are in each of the three cycles. Check
them with someone that you think could add value to you. This
should provide more color and help in your decision-making.

II

The 7 Key Lessons

I extracted the following 7 key lessons from interviews with the Real Estate Titans. I also noticed these same traits with several real estate billionaires that I have either worked for throughout my career or were potential partners or counterparts in different investments in which I have been involved. To ensure that these 7 key lessons were not only my perceptions, but also those of others, I checked this list with three very successful people in different areas of the real estate industry who have personally known several real estate billionaires for years. These three professionals agreed that these 7 lessons represent a distillation of the expansive knowledge and expertise that is shared by those who have achieved notable success in this field.

It is important to understand that these lessons are not meant as individual subject-specific essays but are different facets of the subject matter. There is, by the very nature of the material, some overlap in both example and application. I advise readers to take the 7 lessons as a whole and apply the knowledge in them as needed.

Chapter 12

Key Lesson #1:
A Powerful Mindset

In 2004, Adidas used the slogan "Impossible is Nothing,"[1] excerpted from the following ad copy, to launch a celebrated campaign:

> Impossible is just a big word thrown around by small men who find it easier to live in the world they've been given than to explore the power they have to change it. Impossible is not a fact. It's an opinion. Impossible is not a declaration. It's a dare. Impossible is potential. Impossible is temporary. Impossible is nothing.

Although the campaign was targeted at athletes, the slogan and the ad copy apply to every person in every arena of life. Some people identify this slogan with resolution, others with grit. Whatever you decide to call it, a powerful mindset is the most fundamental trait shared by the world's great—whether they are business leaders, athletes, or Real Estate Titans.

A person with a powerful mindset breaks through the darkest hours on the path to success, a path that was originally thought by others to be too difficult. A powerful mindset keeps the Real Estate Titans from giving up. It gives them the personal vision to pursue their vision, their dream. It's what drives their relentless pursuit to carry out their mission and make an impact on the world.

For Rohit Ravi, a powerful mindset is being able to develop an island in the middle of the Indian Ocean—no matter what extreme challenges arise. From having to ship in all the construction materials, to experiencing delays caused by stormy weather, to training a world-class staff. This requires enormous self-belief.

For Elie Horn, a powerful mindset means gaining knowledge and seeking inspiration. It means never becoming contented and taking life for granted, but always being prepared for the unexpected, for the coming downturn, for the inevitable cycles of the economy.

In Richard Mack's case, his mindset is powerful because he believes in himself and in his vision for what's possible. For him that means finding deals in Eastern Europe that very few others identified and having the courage to pursue this opportunity.

For Carlos Betancourt, a powerful mindset comes from powering through the many difficulties that arise when carrying out land assemblages and looking to redevelop the entire block and help thousands of people with jobs, taxes, new infrastructure and more. It is not giving up when the local government does not supporting the development and eve the neighbors resist. It is doing the impossible and ensuring your vision comes to fruition.

Gina Diez Barroso's mindset is powered by having reasons that push the limits of the status quo. She is striving to change the way things have always been done to find the way it can be done exponentially better. No matter what others say about the difficulties, none of their noise dissuades her.

All these Titans have, at different points in their careers, been told it cannot be done: It's too hard; it's too competitive. They did not listen to these small voices, but persevered and found a way. If they believe they are going to succeed by pursuing an opportunity, "no" is not an acceptable answer to them. The moment that you acknowledge that a problem is unconquerable, you will fail. If you understand that there must be a solution, you will usually find it. Remember that the impossible can only be achieved by those who believe anything is possible.

Perfection in California

Disneyland (in Anaheim, California) occupies approximately 100 acres (400,000 square meters) of land and receives around 18 million visitors per year. Did you know that not too far away from Disneyland, in Los Angeles, there is a shopping center called The Grove that occupies approximately 25 acres (100,000 square meters) of land and receives over 19 million visitors per year? When I first heard these numbers, I was mystified.

How could a little shopping center attract more visitors than the "happiest place on earth?" I soon made a point to get familiar with the owner of The Grove, Rick Caruso,[2] to understand what he and his team did to create the second most successful shopping center in the United States (and the world) in terms of sales per square foot.[3]

Before developing The Grove in the early 2000s, Caruso was told by numerous other market players, consultants, and close colleagues that he should not pursue this opportunity because he would fail. Some said it was on the wrong side of the street. Others said that he was too close to Beverly Center in L.A., which at that time was one of the most dominant shopping centers in California. Others added that there was no need for more retail in the area; L.A. had enough shopping centers.

Instead of listening to so many limiting beliefs, he went to study high shopping streets around the world. Why? Because he knew history. He knew that the Champs Elysees in Paris became a high street, by definition, in the late 1700s, and it has been around— blossoming—since then. That means it has endured the world's greatest wars, famines, plagues, the Great Depression, civil clashes, global recessions, and more. That could also mean it will endure Amazon, e-commerce, social commerce, virtual reality, 3-D printing, and all other future technologies.

Caruso worked with talented architects to extrapolate the most attractive and comforting elements from other beautiful streets such as King Street in Charleston and Newbury Street in Boston. He knew that there was enough retail in Los Angeles but he also knew that there were not enough fun experiences. He therefore focused on creating a shopping center with memorable features, a higher level of customer service, and great operations. He invested in dancing fountains, old-fashioned street trolleys, a concierge service, impeccable bathrooms, and much more.

He never listened to competitors who continually criticized him during the construction period; he knew that it was possible. Massive success was the only option for him.

The Power of the Mind

Think about Richard Ziman starting off his career in the legal practice. There were lots of other real estate lawyers working in Los Angeles and in the state of California. Many graduated from the same law school (University of Southern California) that he did. They had access to similar people; the law was the same for all of them. They each had similar technical skillsets. So why did he succeed in real estate by leaps over all of his peers? One of the main reasons is that he had the mindset to go past the basic expectations.

As you study Richard Ziman you can see that after years of preparing and working for massive success in real estate, he was ready for whatever was thrown at him. He embraced the many different variables that could change because he knew he had no option but to get the end result he was pursuing.

Every other Real Estate Titan has a similar mindset—an insatiable hunger to achieve, to succeed, to keep learning, to change the lives of millions, and to give more.

Many of these individuals—began to develop a mindset at an early age, when it was deeply engrained in their core that one day they would be successful. They were convinced that their eventual success was as real as their need to breathe. They envisioned their success already happening.

They have also learned to control their emotions. This is especially relevant on days when there are big negotiations and closings. They maintain their cool. They don't allow themselves to become emotionally attached to projects. They have a deep understanding of who they are and what they want. They are aware that emotions can cloud their judgment and cause them to overlook or even ignore important data that could derail a deal. They understand that negative thoughts are simply thoughts with no intrinsic power. While negative thoughts and emotions can cause most people to make mistakes and use poor judgment, the Real Estate Titans have learned how to deal with them in a productive way.

Food for Thought

According to research by Dr. Fred Luskin of Stanford University, a human being has approximately 60,000 thoughts per day. And, 90 percent of these thoughts are repetitive. That means we have around 42 thoughts per minute. Most of our thoughts are inaccurate and negative. Most of our thoughts are about tomorrow or yesterday. We masticate on what has happened or meditate on what might happen. We are continually processing ideas, opinions, facts, and choices, and this overwhelming flow of information can be exhausting.

In addition, the average number of decisions the average adult makes each day, according to Stanford, is about 35,000. The steady flow of thoughts often prevents us from listening, seeing, feeling and reacting in ideal ways. Our mind is like a computer, constantly analyzing, reviewing, and replaying information.

According to Dr. Joseph Dispenza, an internationally recognized lecturer on neurosciences, our brain processes 400 billion bits of information a second; but, we are only aware of 2,000 of these. The brain does what it is told, and one of the biggest obstacles to success is a confession of being "less than" what is required to achieve our goals. How many times have you heard someone say, "I don't have the ability to do that" or "I am not smart enough." How many times have you said this throughout your life?

We all feel that our mind sometimes plays tricks on us. Take a look at Figure 12.1. Most real estate entrepreneurs who saw this drawing agreed with it. How could there be so much volatility in one day? Because of our mind. If we develop powerful mindsets we will develop a powerful business and a powerful life.

All the Titans I know have taught themselves to stop overthinking and move forward. Doing so allows them to assess any situation faster and make key decisions in a smarter and more well-balanced manner.

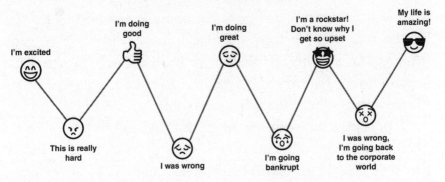

Figure 12.1   The ups and downs of an entrepreneur's day.

Habits That Help the Mind

We all know so many people who are extraordinary talents, very smart individuals with strong technical skills, yet they are not successful in business. How come? When it comes to rising to the top, talent, smarts, and skills are a part of the formula, but the powerful mindset is essential. But this mindset does not come naturally for most people for diverse reasons. Therefore, it is important to learn some of the things that these Real Estate Titans do to stay at the top.

Several of the Titans shared with me that they meditate. Meditation helps to calm your mind so that you can become aware of your emotions, ideas, and thoughts. There are several different types of meditation but they all help reduce stress and anxiety while giving you time alone to get to know yourself a little better. Guided meditation apps have become a popular for the novice who wants to learn about technique and for the experienced practitioner as well.

Most of the Titans have an exercise regimen. We all know exercise has benefits, but let's review some of them to see how they affect brain chemistry and attitude. Exercise increases heart rate and improves the lungs' ability to expel toxins and take in more oxygen.

This promotes the flow of oxygenated blood to the brain. It can improve brain function and protect memory and thinking skills.[4] It has also been shown to cause the hippocampus, a part of the brain that's vital for memory and learning, to grow in size.[5] This serves to increase mental function in older adults. Exercise can also stimulate the production of hormones that enhance the growth of brain cells.

The Titans implement digital detox. A study by Qualtrics and Accel found that Millennials check their phones over 150 times per day. These Titans check their phones and emails significantly less than this and they have numerous hours where they block cell phones, tablets, and computers. This helps them concentrate and experience less stress.

They have also made reading quality newspapers, books, magazines, and industry newsletters an important part of their daily routine. Taking time to read offline can also be a way to relax and yet stimulate your capacity for learning; it can actually improve your mind's ability to receive and optimally process information, making it easier to retrieve when needed.

Many start their day with gratitude and prayer. When they wake up they look in the mirror and acknowledge the many blessings that have manifested in their lives. They realize they have abundance not just in terms of comfort for themselves and their families, but also as a result of making the world a better place for others. They thank God. Titans share the primary mission of leaving a legacy for the benefit of humanity. Many of them will make positive affirmations aloud while preparing for the day. Going forth with this attitude, they find they don't complain about the little things or victimize themselves. This notion of gratitude equips them with a great optimistic attitude.

Every Titan possesses a strong self-belief. You need to believe you can succeed before success can manifest in your life. When you do, your thoughts influence your behavior and actions.

Key Takeaways

- Embrace the mindset that "impossible is nothing."

- Next time you face what seems an insurmountable challenge, ask yourself what would need to happen for this to become possible. What can I do to make this happen? What would one of these Real Estate Titans do? You will surprise yourself if you try and follow their mindset.

- If you are a real estate entrepreneur looking to be successful, you must have a strong mind that can handle the ups and downs of the entrepreneurial pilgrimage. A weak mind is vulnerable to making bad decisions if fear sets in, or when too much information becomes overwhelming. Adopt these habits that Titans have to experience professional growth.

Exercise

Try to think of three people you know who you believe have a powerful mindset. Invite them for lunch or a coffee and ask them to tell you how they have grown to develop such a powerful mindset. Listen to what they tell you and take notes. Once they realize that you truly respect what they have to say and are serious about learning from them, people will often open up and share their experiences and the lessons they have learned from their unique journey. Learn from them. Make a list of the key points and commit them to memory.

Realize that your mentor has added value to your life and be grateful. Look for ways to repay them by adding value to their lives. Pay it forward when you are asked the same.

Notes

1. For a brief history of the Adidas campaign, the ad copy, and the slogan, see https://quoteinvestigator.com/2017/11/28/impossible-is/.

2. Please note that Rick Caruso was not interviewed for this book; however, I have had the pleasure of meeting him and I think that—besides being one of the best real estate developers in the United States—he has a story and a way of thinking that is worth studying

3. www.Fortune.com.

4. National Center for Biotechnology Information.

5. PERFORM Centre and Psychology Department at Concordia University.

Chapter 13

Key Lesson #2:
The Hardest Workers
in Any Room

A few years ago, I heard one of the most awe-inspiring business stories of my life. Joe Sitt, through his extremely hard work ethic, was able to acquire a renowned property in Manhattan even though he was not the highest bidder. He paid $2 million less than the highest bidder and the owner sold him the property. How is this possible, you may ask? Putting aside the fact the Joe is a credible buyer with a good reputation, it was because he—and other people from his team—called or emailed the seller every day for seven years. For seven years!

Hard work is often mischaracterized as just strenuous physical labor, but it can also be intense dedication, sharpened focus, an intricate study of the capital markets, repeatedly calling a prospect with news of an excellent deal, and so much more.

How many people do you know who would have implemented this superhuman work ethic like Joe and his team did? Odds are, very few people. You see, these Real Estate Titans work *tremendously* hard.

I asked Joe Sitt what had happened in his life to drive him to work so hard. How could someone be motivated to pursue a property for such a long time without giving up? He explained that when he was very young, back in the 1980s, he did a short internship in the real estate department of an Asian manufacturing company, and he got to work in Shanghai, Jakarta, Istanbul, and Manila. One important common characteristic he noticed with the different people from all these different cultures was their extraordinary work ethic. Back then, the economic disparity between the United States and Asia was much more pronounced than it is today, and this left an indelible mark in the core of Joe's heart. If these people who had very little in their lives had such a rigorous work ethic, so would he. He had a new appreciation for the blessed opportunity that he had of growing up in New York City, and he made a promise to himself that would always give a superhuman effort to make things happen for him.

Robert Faith started as a sweat equity partner. He advises everyone entering the real estate business to put in the effort to find amazing deals they could never acquire on their own and bring them to investors. Other people will put in their money if you put in the effort to organize a deal that adds value to the people involved and the community at large.

The Titans are immersed in their work for a long part of the week. Most of them work six to seven days a week. Many of them work while they are on vacation—seeing, learning and strategizing. They work harder than their peers, and with a purpose that aims beyond their own success.

They are relentless in their work ethic; it never stops for them. When important moments show up in their professional lives like raising a new equity fund, taking their company public, or closing on a highly competed portfolio of properties, they will find a way to successfully execute those goals. Dozens—and sometimes hundreds—of serious problems will come up during their endeavors. But they will step up and work for however long it's required of them.

Elie Horn often stayed up all night to close deals when he was getting started. If someone wanted to negotiate a contract at 4:00 a.m., he was there at 4:00 a.m. to close the deal.

Those who don't know these Real Estate Titans sometimes call them lucky. Luck did not lead them to success. They continuously succeed because they have spent thousands of hours honing their craft and preparing for these moments of greatness. Like a top performing athlete in any sport. They demand more of themselves than anyone else could ever demand of them. They are always striving to be the best and continue getting better. Many of them work as hard as or harder now than they did when they were younger. When things get tough and don't go their way, which will happen often, they will wake up earlier and work harder to make sure that they are successful in their mission.

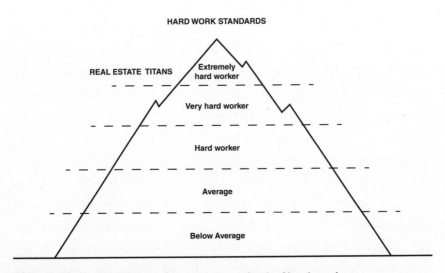

Figure 13.1   Real Estate Titans are not afraid of hard work.

No matter what the weather is like, no matter the time, these men and women are focused on their task at hand. That willingness to work while others are not is one of the differentiating points of those in the 9 and 10 figure clubs.

The paradox is that they don't work because they have to. None of the Titans interviewed in this book need to work for money, they all have total financial freedom. They choose to work because of their love for the game and because of their "why."

They Have a Purpose

What is at the core of these Titans' impressive work ethic? They know why they want to achieve success. Gina Diez Barroso's mindset is powered by having a "why" that is larger than herself. Her reason for working long hours, dividing her time between developer, educator, women empowerer, and full time mother is her goal of having a positive impact on the world. She is striving to change the status quo—the way it's always been done—to the way it can be done exponentially better.

This serves as a great driving force to see every project through to the finish. This is the secret of success for everyone, regardless of profession or field of endeavor. Success is within reach for all who find their "why" in life. Your "why" is what motivates you to go the extra mile, put in the extra effort, and commit to do whatever it takes to achieve your objective.

Many of us find our "why" in providing a better life for our family or sharing opportunity with our friends and neighbors. These Titans are no different from you in that they share this trait and find great happiness and fulfillment in taking care of their spouses and children. They don't live the extravagant lifestyles that one might expect. In fact, these Titans are not interested living in castles or collecting the most elite sports cars. Many of them have devoted a great deal of time enjoying experiences with loved ones that provide inspiration, fulfill personal dreams, and create magical moments.

These Real Estate Titans aren't likely to post their family experiences on Facebook or flaunt them like some celebrities on Instagram. It isn't likely that you will see them making large displays of opulence and extravagance. It is much more likely that you will see them make calculated decisions based on prudence and security. They have learned that value has very little to do with cost.

They understand that the secret to living is giving. They are very active in charitable works and in making an impact on the world that goes much further than their real estate companies or other businesses. This gives them a reason for pushing forward when everyone else has stopped to rest. Titans are pursuing a greater-than-life mission.

Elie Horn, for example, who signed the Giving Pledge originated by Bill Gates Warren Buffett, states: "As human beings, we will carry nothing with us to the other world. The only things we shall take are the good deeds that we accomplish in this world. We are in this world to be tested and each one of us must grant the fruit of his abilities. I make my pledge with pleasure, and the good feeling that I tried my best to give meaning to my mission in this world."

Ronald Terwilliger is a great contributor to a number of different causes, especially affordable housing. He has announced a $100 million legacy gift to Habitat for Humanity and a $5 million gift to the Urban Land Institute to establish the ULI Terwilliger Center for Workforce Housing to aid in housing affordability. He also committed $5 million to Enterprise Community Partners to create 2000 affordable homes annually. The list goes on. "When you're fortunate to build wealth in the housing arena and come from nothing," says Terwilliger. "You have a responsibility to give back to other people."

Chaim Katzman is another great philanthropist. For example, one of his many donations, this one for $25 million, was to build Beit Shulamit (House of Shulamit), a new cancer center in Northern Israel named after his late wife, Dr. Shulamit Katzman, a respected pediatrician and activist in the fight against cancer, who died of the disease herself in 2013.

Every Real Estate Titan in this book is involved in numerous charities and organizations that give them a "why." These are the reasons they jump out of bed in the early morning while most people are still asleep. What is your reason for getting up in the morning?

There are many great books and lots of literature about how to find your "why." But I believe the chart1 shown in Figure 13.2, which illustrates the Japanese term "Ikigai" (literally meaning "reason for being") can serve as a great way to begin finding how to

FIND YOUR WHY

What you love

Passion

Mission

What you're good at

PURPOSE

What the world needs

Profession

Vocation

What you can get paid for

Figure 13.2   Ikigai can help you find your purpose.

identify and direct your passion. Ikigai is about finding fulfillment, happiness, and balance in the daily routine of your life.

Here are four important questions you should ask yourself:

1. What do I love? Is it your passion or do you consider it a mission?
2. What am I good at? Is it something you would do for free, and thus a passion, or is it a profession or vocation?
3. What can I be paid to do it? Is it your profession or vocation, or is it a hobby or creative endeavor?
4. Finally, what does the world need from it? Is it your creative expression or is it, coming full circle, something you feel called upon to do—your mission?

As you answer each question, remember that there may be more than one answer. Don't filter yourself. Use the follow-up questions in each category to determine if an answer is closer to the center of the diagram or further away. Also, use them to determine whether the answer leans more in one direction or the other.

When finished, you will see that you have a scatter diagram. I printed out the diagram and used push-pins to locate my one- or two-word answers. That makes it easy to further define and correlate the data with the next round of qualifiers.

Once you have listed as many interests as you can, try to narrow down further by applying additional qualifiers. Based upon your answer, move the push-pin either closer toward or further away from the center.

- It should be challenging. Your personal Ikigai should lead to mastery and growth.
- It should be your choice. You should have freedom and autonomy as you pursue this calling.
- It should involve an engagement of time and belief.
- It should be something that boosts your well-being by promoting good health, fulfillment, and great relationships.

Passion

The "why" of the Titans cause them to be passionate about the work they do. They don't see it as work but as fun. Richard Mack defines success in world of the real estate as daily doing and *enjoying*—putting in the hard work required to pull together a quality transaction. He calls hard work "fun!"

When these Titans go on trips, they are excited to see other projects, learn from other real estate or business experts, and study innovative elements from around the world. Their endless curiosity drives them to explore and learn new things all the time.

Many of these Titans shared with me that their average wakeup time is 6 a.m., and a few told me they rise before 5 a.m. Several worked throughout their career 16- to 18-hour days and on most weekends. A few attribute a part of their success to working when others don't.

But they don't just work hard; they also work smart and efficiently. Everyone has the same 24 hours in a day to do what needs to be done. Titans try to get the most out of every hour and every day. They understand that it's not just how many hours you spend that matters but also *how* you spend them. It's about achieving objectives and results. Note that this passion is not innate but is something that you can develop, just like muscles develop over time as a result of a prolonged and consistent exercise routine. You develop stamina and endurance when you make a habit of getting out of bed and getting started before your competitors.

The Lesson Kobe Bryant Gave to Jay Williams on Hard Work

Former NBA player (and NCAA star) Jay Williams shared this inspirational story. His team was playing the L.A. Lakers in Los Angeles during the regular season. For Williams this was an important game.

His method for getting mentally and physically prepared for the game was to show up at the arena several hours before the game and shoot around 400 baskets to warm up his body and get mind ready.

The game was scheduled at 7 p.m. As Jay Williams tells it, he shows up at the Staples Center at 3 p.m. He walks onto the floor and there is Laker guard Kobe Bryant already warming up. Jay gets on the court, shoots his baskets, and decides he is done; meanwhile, he sees that Kobe is still working out. He is not shooting the ball in a relaxed way, he is performing game-like moves. Jay sits down to unlace his shoes and see for how long Kobe will keep practicing. After about 25 minutes Jay leaves, Kobe is still on the court.

That night during the game, Kobe destroys Jay and his team. After the game Jay realizes he needs to go ask Kobe why he works out like this and why was he warming up for so long before the game. Kobe replies to him saying, "Because I saw you coming on the court and I wanted you to know that no matter how hard you work that I am going to work harder than you."

Although this is an example from sports it applies perfectly to real estate. The greats watch their competitors. They see the effort they put in and the challenges they overcome. They put in more effort and overcome greater challenges than the competition. That is the work ethic of a Titan.

Geometric Results

I have had the pleasure of knowing numerous real estate leaders who are ultra-high-net-worth individuals. They were all driven by a hunger to achieve many goals throughout their careers, but a few of them at some point got comfortable for different reasons and settled back. They lost some of the hunger, as most people at this level do.

The Real Estate Titans in this book, however, are as hungry today as they were when they started their careers. Some have allowed their success to make them even hungrier. When that hunger never goes away, and individuals pursue their purpose day after day, month after month, year after year, and decade after decade, the level of greatness and the level of results achieved get compounded and the final results are geometric, not incremental. I explain this principle with more detail in Lesson # 4.

Key Takeaways

- Greatness is not something that gets handed to someone; it demands a lot of hard work. The best people in any field are those who devote thousands of hours to their crafts.

- Never stop working for what you want! Failure and rejection are normal first steps on the path to success. The best in the world have failed but they get up and work harder.

- The real estate industry is tough, but you can achieve massive success when you are able to find your "why" and then learn to never give up.

Exercise

Use the Ikigai diagram process to help you determine your "reason for being." Once you have determined it, decide that you are willing to outwork your competitors. As the great British mathematician Lord Kelvin said, "If you cannot measure it, you cannot improve it." This implies that if you can measure it, you can improve your performance. Find the Key Performance Indicators (KPI) for the leading competitors in your market.

They can be metrics such as the average commission per sale, the number of properties advertised per month, the number of funds raised, the yield on cost on current portfolio, the number of homes being flipped, and so on. List as many relevant KPI as you can and make a spreadsheet. Track your performance against those same leaders in your market.

When you consistently track your performance against the leaders in your market, you will find your own performance improving. You will become motivated to work harder. You will begin waking up at 5 a.m. You will find inspiration. Decide you are going to be the best in your market.

Notes

1.   Adapted from Francesc Miralles.

Chapter 14

Key Lesson #3:
Deep Focus and Clarity

In 1979, the students at Harvard Business School were asked, "Have you set clear, written goals for your future and made plans to accomplish them?" Only 3 percent of the graduates had written goals and plans; 13 percent had goals, but they were not in writing; and a whopping 84 percent had no specific goals at all.

Ten years later, the members of the same class were interviewed again and the findings, while somewhat predictable, were nonetheless astonishing. The 13 percent of the class who had goals were earning, on average, twice as much as the 84 percent who had no goals at all. And what about the 3 percent who had clear, written goals? They were earning, on average, 10 times as much as the other 97 percent put together.

Make no mistake: The Titans have very clear goals and objectives. They have them in their head. They have them on paper. They think and dream about them. Their confidantes know them. Setting goals provides long-term vision in their lives. The Titans need powerful, long-range goals to push them toward getting past their short-term challenges. They also love having goals because that pushes them to stretch, grow, and become better.

Goals are a way for you to design your future, instead of leaving it all up to fortune. They help you achieve your highest potential.

Recommendations on Goal Setting

Some important points about goal setting: Goals must be written down. There is something about the act of writing down your goals that seems to set them in motion. A physicist once told me that it has to do with one of the basic rules of physics: Every action has an opposite and equal reaction. The act of physically writing your goals, he explained, set off vibrations in the universe similar to dropping a pebble in a still pond. You are putting the energy out there and it will amplify and come back to you. That may sound like pseudoscience to the uninitiated, but so did the theory of black holes when it was first proposed.

Another useful technique is using the acronym SMART for each goal that you write down. Your goal must be as detailed and as *Specific* as you can make it. Your goal must be *Measurable*. It must be something that is actually *Attainable*. Your goal must be *Relevant* to what you are doing and it must be *Time-bound*. Your goals MUST have a deadline. They need to make you feel uncomfortable when you set them but at the same time, they must be congruent with your core values and beliefs.

For example, one of the Titans shared with me one of his first career goals: "I plan on purchasing a residential property in the next three months (by X date) by raising money from X people that will generate $X amount of cash flow (a 10 percent cash on cash) immediately after acquisition." This is a well-written goal because it is specific, measurable, and attainable—and it has a deadline.

In offline conversations I have had with some of the Titans, they mentioned that real estate goal setting is very important to being successful. Goals push us to believe in ourselves and in our ability to achieve our highest potential. As Napoleon Hill states, "Set your mind on a definite goal and observe how quickly the world stands aside to let you pass."

The Titans also mentioned that you must have someone hold you accountable, because goals are not as powerful if there is no one following up. You must find someone who you think can hold you responsible, like a good friend or colleague you trust, who will repeatedly follow up with you and check on the progress you have made toward reaching your goals.

A Personal Example on the Power of Goals

When I was 10 years old my family took a trip to New York City. I was much shorter back then and the buildings seemed like they reached all the way into the sky. As I walked through the atrium of Trump Tower, a 58-story building sitting in the prime 57th Street and 5th Avenue corner, it became a goal and a dream of mine to one day meet the man with the power to put his name on the front of such a building. Just 16 years later, I ended up working for that very man and his three children, who always treated me with fairness and respect: Ivanka, Don Jr., and Eric. I learned many valuable lessons while working for the family; my three main lessons follow.

1. **Talent is very important.** At the Trump Organization, Donald Trump and his children had a profound notion of hiring the very best talent they could find to get extraordinary results (I discuss this in Lesson #5). At the time I was there, the company had an impressive team of talented and hard-working people in all areas of the real estate business.

2. Marketing is essential in real estate. Peter Drucker, known by many as the father of modern consulting, said long ago that "because the purpose of business is to create a customer, the business enterprise has two—and only two—basic functions: marketing and innovation." While most real estate developers that I know have neglected this premise, Trump has embraced it fully. Donald Trump is arguably the preeminent marketing genius in the world of real estate. From his early days in the business he understood the importance of marketing and of branding, and this was evident to me while at his firm. The Trumps understood who their ideal customer is and have known how to market a product for that client. In some cases, the client is a final user who buys an apartment in one their luxurious buildings, and in other cases it's someone who pays them a hefty sum of money to use their brand for an iconic project in an emerging market.

3. Think big. Donald Trump understood that doing a $20 million development and a $200 million development requires a similar amount of time and effort. Therefore, he chose to think big and do bigger deals. This is the type of thinking that led him to become President of the United States against all odds. This is what has allowed him to expand far beyond real estate and into numerous other businesses that are predominantly successful. Trump taught his children that "there is no such thing as an unrealistic goal, just unrealistic time frames," and this motto was prevalent at all times I interacted with them.

Clarity

Besides having very specific goals, the Real Estate Titans also have remarkable clarity. They grew to be experts either in a specific segment (like shopping centers) or geographical area (like New York City) or an investment type (Mezzanine Financing) because true expertise requires depth.

Although it's possible, it's not advisable for beginners to try and be experts in more than a few segments. If you study the careers of Ronald Terwilliger or Bob Faith, you will note they chose to be preeminent experts in the multi-family sector. Urs Ledermann is an expert within the residential sector in Zurich, Switzerland. Rohit Ravi is an expert in the hotel segment in southern India. Chaim Katzman is a master at acquiring and developing shopping centers. Joseph Sitt is arguably the world's leading authority on high street retail. Richard Ziman is a virtuoso when it comes to office and industrial buildings in California. And the list goes on.

This is true not just of the Titans but also large development groups and investment vehicles such as REITs. The largest and best performing REITs are usually focused on one specific sector. For example, Simon Property Group, one of the biggest REITs in the world, focuses only on retail. Simon explores different niches like open-air fashion malls, power centers, neighborhood centers, out-lets, and more within that segment, but they are only focused on the retail niche. Analysts have historically rewarded Simon for this sector expertise because they understand the complexities involved with trying to be an expert in different niches, segments, and geographies.

Develop a Specific Area of Expertise

As many Titans have recommended, everyone should start in real estate focused on a very specific segment and geography and build their strategy from there.

Real estate is a colossal world comprising so many sectors and niches. While we refer to real estate as an industry, it's not just one industry. It's actually a whole segment of the economy. It includes many distinct businesses like construction, brokerage, private equity, architecture, and so much more, each of which is an industry unto itself. Repositioning office buildings in central business districts, developing world-class hotel resorts, and taking real estate companies public are all different industries, each one with uniquely different fundamentals. Chaim Katzman said in his interview that even though he was a prominent real estate developer, he failed when he delved into the construction sector. Why? Largely because it involves a different economic logic.

Your goal should be to find a category of real estate in your region where you can gain experience and develop expertise as quickly as possible. Do not get caught up in the noise and overwhelmed by all of the information. If you don't know the answer, look for a veteran in your chosen specialty and offer to take that person to lunch, then ask questions about whatever has you puzzled. Eventually you will find someone who will become your guide or mentor. Real estate people, regardless of their specialty, love to share lessons learned in their own careers. Most of them have developed one or two areas of expertise.

You will be able find a niche that appeals to your particular talents. You will have the opportunity to apply your skills, your vision, and your work ethic to make your chosen industry better. Some questions to help you in this quest for the right fit could be: What are your core values? What kind of people do you want to work with? Who do you envision as your final customer? What makes you different? How do others see you? Which asset class would you like to work in? Which geographies do you want to focus on?

Let's assume that you are a real estate agent pitching a potential client on selling a two-bedroom apartment in New York City, but you also represent home sellers in Newark, New Haven, and Albany. Those are four cities in three different states. You would probably be better off being the New York City or Manhattan condo specialist who has sold 23 units in the past four months than being the agent who sells homes everywhere. Some of the reasons for this are the costs of travel between markets, the different networks you have to develop and maintain in each city; the local regulations, which are usually different; the diverse supply and demand fundamentals; and the different tastes and preferences of buyers and renters. In addition, New York City is a big enough market (and arguably the most competitive in the world) for you to get scale and potentially create a large business.

Let's look at a second example: Throughout my career I have been involved in the acquisition, development, and sale of a number of shopping centers. I have seen all kinds —some great ones and others that were unfortunately done without much thought. Specifically, I have seen developers who are experts at building industrial warehouses, residential buildings, or commercial office towers come into the retail space and get destroyed because they forget to focus. Strategic Planning Concepts International, one of the foremost retail experts in the world in my opinion, uses the graph shown in Figure 14.1 to show their clients how to avoid trying to be all things to all people and thus falling into "The Black Hole of Retail."

In other words, they have gotten clients come to them looking to develop shopping centers with big hypermarkets like Walmart, services such as banks and pharmacies, fast-fashion stores like H&M or Zara, entertainment concepts like cinemas and arcades, and luxury brands like Ferragamo or Tiffany, all within the same complex. Does this make sense?

Such a mall may sound crazy to you, but there are thousands of shopping centers around the world where developers wanted to be many things for many people, forgot to push emotion aside, and then failed big time. You must focus and decide what you want to be strongest in. Perhaps it's high quality and entertainment? Perhaps you want to develop an outlet center where you are focused on being the best price? You must choose.

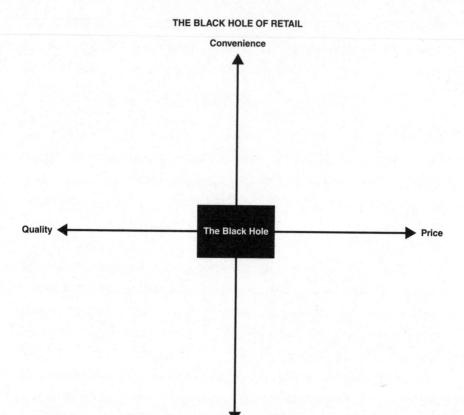

Figure 14.1   Choose one specialty, not all, to avoid falling into the black hole of retail.

Source: Strategic Planning Concepts International.

Developing an area of expertise means that you will say no to many opportunities and deals that come your way in the future. This also means that, as you grow, you will sometimes have to make some people unhappy. Remember that if you want to become an important player in real estate you must be disciplined and adopt a long-term view. Stay focused on your goals. If you have an area of expertise, your ability to command substantial and sustained returns is going to be significantly higher in the long term.

Clarity in Real Estate Investing

If you want to become a real estate investor, Table 14.1 shows the current options you have. As technology continues to evolve there will be new opportunities; however, always remember that because real estate is non-liquid asset class, it is important to invest in properties or vehicles that you know you will be able to one day sell. It is never wise to enter a deal without an exit strategy because situations change in real estate. You need to have situational awareness and know your options at all times.

Table 14.1   Ways to Invest in Real Estate

	Equity	Debt
Private	• Direct investments • Real estate funds • Real estate fund of funds • Real estate foundations • Property investment clubs	• Direct mortgages • Real estate debt foundations • Private real estate debt funds
Public	• Real estate equities • Equity REITs (real estate investment trusts) • Listed real estate funds	• Bonds from real estate companies • Mortgage REITs • Mortgage bonds • Agency mortgage-backed securities • Commercial mortgage-backed securities (CMBSs) • Residential mortgage-backed securities (RMBSs)

Source: Credit Suisse.

Besides knowing what type of investments you want to pursue, it's also important to gain clarity on what kind of investor you are. Some people really love taking on new challenges with a lot of risk. They are optimistic by nature and like to think that rents will grow annually at above inflation prices, that they will be able to obtain financing from a lender with a 75 percent loan-to-value ratio and very attractive debt terms. They believe, despite periodic adjustments, that the market will always go up, and so forth.

Other investors are just the opposite. They are more risk averse and take a more conservative approach to real estate investing. They like to buy assets with very little or no debt. They like to buy at a discount to replacement cost. They like to buy when others are selling. This is something similar to a value-add investor. In this type of investment strategy, the buyer is more focused on finding market imbalances and dislocations. The main idea is that if they can buy at the right price and be disciplined with their debt (let's say 50 percent), no matter how deep the downturn is or how volatile the market becomes, they should still be able to make a profit from their investment.

As you think about the many different routes you can follow for creating your investment strategy, understand that only you can determine which approach is best suited for you.

Time Management and Planning

Anyone who runs a successful real estate business has learned the discipline of putting the majority of their limited time into IPAs— Income Producing Activities. This does not mean that they have no time for pleasurable activities, but they understandably say "no" to many things that the average person considers routine. This is especially true for Titans.

For example, if you are a real estate investor or developer, an important part of the business is walking the property (as well as the neighborhood or district). However, these Titans have to reject many invitations to tour properties, and only see the properties that they are seriously considering buying or investing in, because their time is so limited.

In fact, as I wrote this book I reached out to approximately 50 different Real Estate Titans for interviews, and most of them said that they wanted to participate in the book but couldn't afford to grant me the time. Others said that they would participate in the book but that I should reach out in a few months because their schedules were already booked. One person told me that they wanted to participate in the book but could only do so in 12 months—12 months! As ridiculous as that might sound, these Titans have incredible regard for their time. Money comes and goes but time can never be recovered. Titans are experts at saying no to most people because they just don't have enough time in the day.

How do you learn to plan like a Real Estate Titan? Be focused and disciplined. Fill out your calendar for the week or month and write down when you will do what, and how. At the end of each day reflect on what you have learned and in what areas you could improve. What are some things to do?

1. **Prioritize your objectives.** Determine what is most important for you to accomplish in your day/month/year and stay focused until you achieve it.
2. **Prioritize your list daily.** Be honest and revalue your objectives. Learn to say no—a lot—and eliminate unproductive items from your daily to-do list.
3. **Be disciplined with your email and use of your social media**. Choose a few hours during the day to answer emails and social media messages. Do not carry out these

endeavors throughout the entire day because they will continually distract[1] you.

4. **Create written agendas for meetings and share with the participants, and then follow it closely.** This will help you stay on track and avoid wasting time. Seasoned real estate professionals will recognize that you value their time as much as you do your own. Earning their respect will pay big dividends over the course of your career.

Lessons on Focus in Development from Ronald Terwilliger

Ronald Terwilliger believes it's very important to choose a core competency in real estate, especially in the earlier stages of your career when you have less experience. In his words:

> Companies that restrict their development to a single product line, such as rental apartments, are able to develop a core competency in financing, design, construction, and leasing.
>
> While there are always subtle differences across markets, I felt more comfortable being able to evaluate new development risks for rental apartments, since I had done this type of development across hundreds of projects.
>
> To avoid mistakes related to the local nature of development, my company (Trammell Crow Residential) embraced local partners who lived in the local community. We tried to have the best of both worlds by having both geographic diversity and local partners who could bring important local knowledge to the process.

An advantage for developers with a product focus is the ability to credibly participate in each part of the business cycle by raising funds for rehab (value added) as well as acquisitions during parts of the business cycle in which development is not feasible.

Ronald Terwilliger also believes that if you are in the development or repositioning game, you should always use architects and/or subcontractors who are familiar with the product type you are building. Terwilliger believes that one of the biggest dangers in development is delving into other niches that you don't know very well, only to have your construction firm make mistakes that cause cost overruns, wasted time, and lost opportunities.

A Story of Focus

Zhang Xin is an icon and billionaire in China. Even though I did not interview her for this book, I would like to use her story to exemplify the power of clarity and focus.

Zhang Xin grew up in the 1960s in Communist China under the reign of Mao Zedong. She was born into a low-class family when it was widely believed that there was no greater calling than to be a "peasant."

She yearned for a world of beauty and color. Moving to Hong Kong with her family showed her a world of lights, chromaticity, and beauty. At the time, Hong Kong was still under British control, and this gave Zhang unique access to the British educational system. She leveraged her passions into a scholarship to study economics in England, and after graduating from university went to work in the London office of Goldman Sachs.

A few years later on a trip to visit China, she met her future husband, Pan Shiyi, which motivated her to return home. Pan Shiyi was a real estate developer who had never left China. He managed to steal her heart, proposing only four days after they met.

Like many couples in love, they decided to go into business together. They created SOHO, a property development firm with a very specific focus in sector and geography. While they started off in residential buildings, today SOHO only develops vertical office buildings (sometimes with a retail component in the bottom) within the central business districts of Beijing and Shanghai. In addition, their business model is based on the fact they sell their floors to individual tenants instead of leasing the whole building to one or two large corporate owners. That way, they differentiate themselves from many other developers who build office buildings to lease and own the buildings long-term. Nestled within a very specific niche of a specific segment and geography, SOHO China has successfully developed over 60 million square feet and collaborated with world-renowned architects like Zaha Hadid to create iconic, tech-forward landmark buildings.

When you have laser focus and clarity, you tend to create your own market niche.

Key Takeaways

- Understand the importance of goals.
- Choose to become an expert on one sector and/or geographical area. The Titans grew to be experts in a specific segment (like developing residential), geographical area (like Los Angeles), and/or investment type (equity) because true expertise requires depth.

- Remember that while we refer to real estate as an industry, it's not just one industry. It's many industries and you have to choose the one you want to get involved in. Consider the many different routes available and choose an approach that you believe is best suited for you.

- Be very picky and careful with your time because it is your most valuable asset. Money will come and go but time will not. Therefore, be organized and create a calendar to organize what you think is the best use of your time.

Exercise

Write down three goals that you have for this month, for the coming 3 months, and for the next 12 months. Be as specific as possible. Review them every single day.

Notes

1. Every single Titan I interviewed was present (totally focused), and remained uninterrupted by important emails or phone calls, for the length of the interview.

Chapter 15

Key Lesson #4: Educated and Quantitative

S am Walton, the founder of Walmart, went to Brazil many years ago to meet with businessmen. He got arrested in the process. The cops thought he was a danger to society because they found him on his hands and knees, measuring the amount of space a store had between its aisles. Even though he was the richest man in the United States at the time this happened, Sam Walton had the modest attitude to understand that there was always more he could learn from competitors and businesses all over the world.

These Titans all recognize that the world is simply too vast for them to have a complete understanding of it. They are intellectually curious, and they consistently seek to feed their minds with valuable information.

While some of these Titans have prestigious college or master's degrees, many do not. Their education did not come from school or university but from life experiences, and by learning from others who already achieved their goals.

Read

We live in a time when education is on the decline. Many people decide to stop learning new things when they graduate, whether it's from high school, university, or a postgraduate program. Even more are being graduated from high schools across the country having never really learned how to learn.

There is an old Native American saying that translates: "The day you stop learning is the day you start dying." One of your most important deliberate decisions should be to continue educating yourself. There is always something new to learn. Many of the individuals interviewed in this book started their careers before the home computer even existed. If they chose not to learn how to use this tool or the smartphone, they might not be at the top today. They continually improve, and so should you.

Remember that in life you develop a passion for things that you have interest in and that you are educated about. The more you know about a certain field the more you are likely to enjoy it.

Every single Titan I interviewed reads at least one major newspaper every morning; a few read up to four. Many subscribe to world-class newsletters like *The Memos with Howard Marks* at Oaktree Capital Management or Byron Wien's *Market Commentary* at Blackstone. There are many other newsletters and you should read some of these to get a well-rounded view of where the market is and where it is likely to go.

The Titans join think tanks, Fortune 500 boards, private clubs, and other groups where they get to exchange ideas with elite thinkers. I have heard the finance and real estate expert Bill Ackman say on two different occasions that many of his investment ideas come from reading the *Wall Street Journal*. Exchanging words with Ronnie Chan, a real estate mogul in China, he said that he has gotten valuable business ideas from reading the newspaper.

But it isn't just about reading the financial and real estate news. Being a world-class real estate investor requires creativity, which comes from understanding many fields and connecting ideas. These Titans are intellectually curious, asking lots of questions and going down different avenues of learning to expand their minds.

For instance, Bob Faith read a book by a healthcare consultant, which gave him instrumental ideas about how to carry out the property management in his real estate portfolio. He did not go out and find this information intentionally. It was serendipitous happenstance.

As our Titans have repeatedly shared, some of their best business decisions have come from noticing changes in the market before everyone else. Find a source of news that will give you an advantage over your competitors. As different news sources lead either to the left or the right, you need to find the truth somewhere in between. More important than the daily stories you read are the trends you'll notice. With the amount of information available to us in this digital age, it's possible to become an expert in diverse business arenas without ever setting foot in the classroom.

If all your information is only confined to one field or industry, you will probably be lacking perspective. This is especially true in today's global interconnected world. Anyone willing to look can get new-found perspectives from books, other literature, and people.

Doing so can also help you find anomalies or disruptions in an industry, in a specific market, in a city or neighborhood, or in a particular company. Recognizing the psychology of extremes in markets can lead to attractive entry points.

Search your local or university library for thought-provoking books. Subscribe to high quality magazines such as the *Economist*, the *New Yorker*, the *Atlantic*, and so forth. Read newspapers such as the *Wall Street Journal*, the *Financial Times*, and the *New York Times*. Search documentaries. Search the internet. Scroll through your LinkedIn contacts and read the articles and blogs they post there. Each resource is full of opportunities for intellectual feasting. As an example, Ray Dalio, arguably the greatest financial investor of all time and founder of Bridgewater Associates, recently shared this in a LinkedIn post about acquiring knowledge.

"Learning must come before deciding. Your brain stores different types of learning in your subconscious, your rote memory bank, and your habits. No matter how you acquire your knowledge or where you store it, what's most important is that what you know paints a true and rich picture of the realities that will affect your decision."[1]

He also recommends that every person read the following four books:[2]

1. *The Hero with a Thousand Faces* by Joseph Campbell
2. *The Lessons of History* by Will and Ariel Durant
3. *River Out of Eden* by Richard Dawkins
4. *Super Mind* by Norman Rosenthal

Feed Your Mind with History

What would happen if we all kept up an accelerated learning curve for the rest of our lives, and continued to read thought-provoking books and articles? The world would probably be a much more competitive place. If you are reading this then it's because you *do* have the desire to continue educating yourself, to develop new skills and capacities. Therefore, I would ask you to do what the Titans recommend, to be that unusual person with an appetite for finding new ideas and solutions.

Ronald Terwilliger states that after around 50 years in the development business, he noticed that very few development companies spent much time and energy encouraging their teams to analyze historical supply and demand trends. Only during a recession, once supply started to exceed demand due to overbuilding, and their businesses started to suffer, did they began to question the development business model. He therefore recommends studying past economic and real estate cycles to learn what not to do. Be a student of history.

Rohit Ravi studied the history of India. He studied the stories of real estate within South India by reading books and speaking to other experienced and knowledgeable people. He knows when recessions began and when they ended. He knows when there were booms and when they ended because everything got priced in. He knows about the bull markets in real estate and the bear markets. He knows when there were wars and panics in India; he learned how market players and final customers reacted during those times. Because emotions take over during those moments, he learned that these patterns will likely repeat themselves. He also learned that you need to understand the business environments and you must have a vision of the future. However, to think of the future, you should also know the past.

So, what are some good questions you can ask yourself when you are studying real estate history? Why did this downturn occur six years ago in the market and what can be learned from it? Can I draw any general or specific conclusions? What are some of the common characteristics of successful developers in this industry? What about developers? Why did some large real estate companies fail in this market or at this time, and what can I learn from that? What are some recurring patterns in this market or within my specific niche? How have zoning laws changed? How has that specific city grown?

Remember that we cannot predict the future, but we can learn from the past. We can learn what worked, what didn´t work, and why it didn't work.

Numbers, Back of the Envelope (BOTE) Analysis, and Spreadsheets

Real estate is, in large part, a numbers game. Without fail, every Real Estate Titan I interviewed in this book said the same thing. In addition, every Titan I have ever worked for or done business with is quantitative. This is not to say that they run advanced calculus in their head, but they do have a strong grip of the basic numbers that matter, such as potential sales or rents, development costs, operating costs, capital expenditures, going in and exit cap rates, margins, discount rates, internal rates of return, and so forth.

A few of the Titans confessed to starting off their careers without mathematical skills, but through their hunger and curiosity, they learned quickly. They did this by immersing themselves in numbers and surrounding themselves with advisers and successful players to help them develop this skill. Like most things in life, you need to practice, and the more numbers you analyze the better you can become.

One thing to note about spreadsheets and other analytical tools, they are only as good as the assumptions you include in them. What I mean is that spreadsheets can provide us whatever results we want and therefore the assumptions that we are projecting will eventually determine how close we are to reality. When we analyze real estate, we must be cold and neutral and not succumb to our desires of wanting to do the deal for personal interest or emotional reasons.

One of the most useful tools that allows all the Titans to quickly examine the hundreds of investment opportunities they are offered is a Back of the Envelope (BOTE) analysis. What exactly is a BOTE analysis?

It is a relatively simple mathematical computation that uses numerical assumptions to quickly develop a ballpark figure of the types of returns you could expect if you invest in that specific property or investment opportunity. It purposefully does not have too much detail so that you can quickly arrive at a preliminary conclusion and see if the opportunity passes the "smell test."

While the process may seem over simplistic or inaccurate—especially to young investment bankers who are absolute experts at creating sophisticated excel models with incomprehensible formulas and multiple sensitivities—it fulfills its purpose. Most of the time, these complex excel models are not necessary because property level analysis is not advanced science.

Let's run through the main elements required for a BOTE analysis of an existent commercial property. The main assumptions are:

- the purchase price of the property and all closing costs;
- the amount of equity required, and how it will be invested;
- the loan amount, main terms, disbursements, and repayment schedule;
- the monthly rental income and operating expenses; and
- the exit cap rate.

Assume that we are looking to purchase a Class B multifamily building in the outskirts of Cincinnati, Ohio: a 100-unit property (70,000 square feet of leasable space) that is selling for $9.6 million. The property is at 95 percent occupancy and is producing $600,000 in annual revenues and has operating expenses of \$120,000. Therefore, it has a net operating income of \$480,000.

- **Net Operating Income = Total Revenues − Operating Expenses**

Because we know that occupancy for the past six years has averaged 95 percent, we are comfortable leaving this assumption untouched and do not assume any increase. We also know that current rents in the building are at market.

As we look at the local market info and speak to different local brokers, we notice that the going cap rate of 5 percent is a little higher than market comps (between 5.75 and 6.75 percent) and the acquisition price per unit of \$96,000 is also a little higher than recent transactions (note that in multifamily projects "price per unit" is often used as a metric). In addition, because we know that two lenders in the area are willing to finance 60 percent of the transaction at an all-in cost of 5 percent, we realize that the increased leverage would not increase our returns but would decrease the required equity.

There are two additional things that we come to learn as we continue our analysis. The first is that these trusted brokers tell us that a new university is opening this year a few miles away, and this will cause net operating income to increase in the coming year by around 8 percent. They base this assumption on a similar situation that occurred in nearby cities.

The second thing is that the building will require an immediate capital expenditure investment of \$1.5 million according to a local civil engineer expert that already analyzed the property (this is normal since the building is 15 years old). The good thing about these capital expenditures is that they will have to be done in common areas like the pool and gym, so the apartments will go unharmed and can continue with their high occupancy.

If we add these two variables to our analysis, then we can assume that the property will cost $10.6 million and will produce a net operating income of $518,400. Therefore, this would represent a going-in cap rate of around 4.9 percent. This would mean that if we were interested in obtaining financing we would have negative leverage, something that is not recommendable.

As we analyze this deal, it is also important to examine the acquisition cost versus the replacement cost. We know that our cost is approximately $151 per leasable square foot. However, the trusted brokers and an engineer told us that the replacement cost is at $120 per square foot.

With the information at hand, we can conclude that this deal is not too interesting, and we can either put it on hold for now or we can discard it. However, the intent of this analysis is to show you a way in which the Titans analyze real estate deals.

Although the Titans are experts in BOTE analysis, there are also many situations in which a more detailed pro forma is required, especially if you have more variables and want to run different scenarios. The uses of a spreadsheet analysis are as follows:

For ground up development of commercial real estate, you can see the changes in:

- development costs (land, construction, and soft costs);
- income and occupancies;
- operating expenses;
- reserves and capital expenditures; and
- sale assumptions (exit cap rates).

For acquisition of commercial real estate, you can see the changes in:

- acquisition costs;
- income and occupancies;
- operating expenses;
- reserves and capital expenditures; and
- sale assumptions (exit cap rates).

For ground-up development for sale properties, you can see the changes in:

- development costs (land, construction, and soft costs);
- sale prices of units; and
- velocity and timing of sales.

In all the above scenarios, spreadsheets can help you analyze equity and debt needs, financing terms and draws, refinancing terms and costs, tax effects and benefits, dividend and waterfall distributions to partners, and returns and equity multiples.

A note about financial models and spreadsheets that the Titans know all too well: Because they are usually projected to have between 7 and 10 years, spreadsheets assume that there will always be an increase in rents and expenses. However, this is likely not the reality because there will be years in which rents will not rise but will fall. This is true even when you have long-term leases in place.

Why? Imagine that you have a large tenant like Nike renting a space in your office building and they have a 10-year lease in place but in year 3 you all get hit with a hard recession. During that time it is likely that Nike will ask to renegotiate the lease because numerous other building owners are offering them better space on that same block for a lower rent. Most large tenants will renegotiate lease terms (including rents) during downturns and you have to be ready for this. The moral is therefore to be aware of your assumptions and to run several different downside scenarios. What happens if rents go down by 5 percent? What happens if your occupancy decreases from 95 to 87 percent?

Taxes

An important note on taxes: This book is written for readers from all around the world and therefore does not cover any tax discussion or fiscal issues. Like real estate, the tax code is local, and it is essential for you to begin learning about these codes and fiscal strategies as they pertain to real estate in your city. I would highly recommend you surround yourself with a good tax strategist to help you see how you can save on taxes and create structures that make sense. The bigger a player you are in real estate, the more savings you can have by creating smart tax strategies and structures before making an investment. These savings can result in years of work.

Asymmetric Risk Reward

As you become more educated and develop your quantitative skills, you will also become better at identifying asymmetric risk reward opportunities.

The traditional theory in real estate might seem that you must take on a lot of risk to get high returns. But savvy investors believe quite the contrary. In fact, they usually get higher returns by taking on much less risk.

So how do they do this? In simplified terms, they do this by making investments they believe have small risks but potentially big rewards. Because they are very active buyers when everyone else is desperate to sell, they can find bargains. They find investments with strong fundamentals that might look like bad deals at the current time of acquisition, but that with some small changes should ultimately be worth significantly more than what they are paying for it. See the hypothetical example in Figure 15.1:

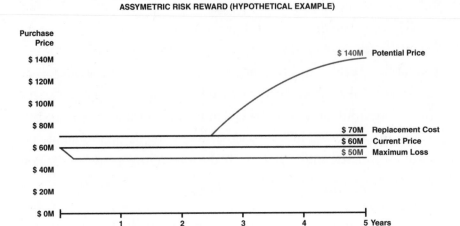

Figure 15.1   A small risk can yield a big reward.

In this simple example, investors would be willing to buy at $60 million because they are buying below replacement cost, they have little risk, and they believe that in a few years the price will go to $140 million with some small operational changes. Therefore, they could make $80 million in profit. They also believe that their loss is capped to only $10 million in case of a maximum loss. This approach of 8 to 1 should be very appealing to any investor. See Appendix B for an example of a value-add investment.

Understanding Geometric Returns

These Titans understand the power of compounding. I assume that you also do, but just in case you don't I think it would be good to give an example.

Many years ago, a real estate tycoon shared with me an intriguing story that taught me many things about the effects of compounding. For privacy reasons, we will call this person James. Through his relationship with a prominent landowner, James was able to negotiate the acquisition of an off-market vacant property that had residential zoning. Specifically, the landowner could develop two residential towers intended for sale in the outskirts of a very large city in a developing market.

Because he had an investor base from past projects he had built, James was able to place a very small deposit to secure the site, let's assume this amount was $1 (see Figure 15.2). He then had 60 days to turn around with his investors and raise the required equity to buy the property, and have as well some working capital for initial

THE POWER OF COMPOUNDING

Quarter 1	$ 1 Day 1 Investment
Quarter 2	$ 2
Quarter 3	$ 4
Quarter 4	$ 8
Quarter 5	$ 16
Quarter 6	$ 32
Quarter 7	$ 64
Quarter 8	$ 128
Quarter 9	$ 256
Quarter 10	$ 512
Quarter 11	$ 1,024
Quarter 12	$ 2,048
Quarter 13	$ 4,096
Quarter 14	$ 8,192
Quarter 15	$ 16,384
Quarter 16	$ 32,768
Quarter 17	$ 65,536
Quarter 18	$ 131,072
Quarter 19	$ 262,144
Quarter 20	$ 524,288
Quarter 21	$ 1,048,576
Quarter 22	$ 2,097,152
Quarter 23	$ 4,194,304
Quarter 24	$ 8,388,608

Figure 15.2   Earnings generate more earnings over time.

requirements such as design and permits. After he succeeded raising this initial capital, he focused on creating some preliminary designs with a local architecture firm and on obtaining the construction license. James also hired a marketing firm (that he would pay in case the project closed) to help him create some marketing materials to start selling the condos.

After accomplishing these diverse feats, James sat down with other investors that he knew and sold most of the units in this project to finance the entire development. Because he had a good reputation he convinced his investors that this was a very attractive opportunity to obtain high returns (+30% IRRs), and his company would be in charge of construction and development. James was charging a structuring fee as well as a series of development fees. In a period of six years (24 quarters) he made several million dollars with a $1 investment. Every quarter his money doubled. This is, of course, far from a typical return, but James managed to achieve this.

Please note that this example is very specific to emerging markets because in most of these countries you can pre-sell condominiums in developments and use that money to finance the construction. This is not the case in advanced economies like the United States, where the money has to be placed in escrow in order to protect the buyer and ensure that in case the developer does not finish construction, they return the money to buyers.

This example above shows how the power of compounding creates a snowball effect that occurs when earnings generate more earnings. You can receive interest not only on your original investment, but also on the dividends and capital gains that accumulate. Therefore, your investment can grow faster and faster as the months and years go by.

This concept is very important to understand because it can significantly change your point of view regarding when you should invest, how you should invest, and in what you should invest. The power of compounding is also one of the reasons why experienced real estate players see this asset class as a long-term investment.

Prepare for Downturns

A successful real estate player is one who can ask the right questions and understand how to mitigate the risk. Make sure you research your market until you comprehend which elements (micro and/or macro) are affecting your investment. With enough knowledge, you'll begin noticing patterns and trends before your competitors. This type of understanding can lead to better decision-making and planning for the future—like preparing for a sellers' market when you recognize the signals for one.

In real estate, no matter where you are in the world, the volume of development and acquisitions is related to the availability of funds, not to demand. You need to understand demand, but unfortunately many real estate players are not rational. Real estate markets have a history of overbuilding when there's easy money, without regard for who will occupy those spaces once they're built. Therefore, be cautious and think of all the potential downsides.

Economic downturns are inevitable. History confirms this. The Titans confirm this. We know downturns will come, but we don't know when they will happen. To prepare for future economic downturns, look at the economic downturns of the past. What caused them? Which businesses collapsed? Which businesses thrived?

Study the choices that separated the winners from the losers and implement those in your real estate strategy. This means finding and developing income streams for tough times. Part of this preparation entails always looking at the downside of any project or real estate investment before you proceed. Ask yourself two very simple questions: What would have to happen for this project to fail? Where is demand coming from?

A Note on Financing

As you think about developing an advanced quantitative skillset, know that becoming a master in financing is a must.

Chaim Katzman shared his points of view on financing. One of his important recommendations is to keep relatively low leverage on deals (or in case you have a company, on its balance sheet) and have a lot of equity.

Financing can seem complicated when you first enter the world of real estate, but the rule of thumb is that when most financial entities are not willing to lend you money, it's a good time to use leverage.

In real estate, consider downturns and recessions as imminent. You need to be ready for a recession on any given day. You need to have your leverage at such a level that you can comfortably survive a two- or three-year period of difficulties.

How can you do this? With long-term debt locked in, as well as available lines of credit that can act as shock absorbers to fill the gaps in times when the capital markets are open for refinancing. The line of credit is meant to help you breach periods when the capital markets are not open. Look at what happened to General Growth Properties, a large shopping center REIT that almost failed during the great recession of 2008. Between 2004 and 2008, they spent $7.2 billion in cash to acquire a bunch of shopping malls and a famous land development company. By 2008, General Growth owed more than $25 billion and didn't have enough liquidity to make the debt payments. They were illiquid. In the real estate business having some liquidity is of crucial importance.

What do banks love the most when it comes to real estate? Having really good assets, of course, ones that suffer the least during downturns and generate the cash flows that keep the lending institutions and bond holders very calm. These players know that the cash flows will be there to service the loans in a timely manner.

Chaim Katzman also addressed the issue of personal liability and strongly recommended against it. As you study real estate history, you can note that in the 1980s in the United States, a lot of investors and developers got into trouble by agreeing to recourse financing, allowing the bank to access not only the property put up as collateral but also other assets the borrower owns.

As Ron Terwilliger also pointed out, "Banks are the ultimate fair-weather friends. When you're borrowing from a bank and things are going well, they're your best friends—they're happy to give you money, and they want to be in a partnership with you. But when things get tough—when there's a recession or a downturn in the market—banks begin to think like machines. They are no longer your friends."

Key Takeaways

- Subscribe to one high-quality newspaper (like the *Wall Street Journal* or the *New York Times*) and try to read it every day. Look for daily updates on websites for respected weekly magazines like the *Economist*. This will expand your mind and help you come up with new ideas.

- It is important you develop quantitative skills. If you don't have a quantitative skillset, you can go to Real Estate Financial Modeling, a company founded by Bruce Kirsch, who is an expert in teaching people the necessary financial skills for success in real estate. He agreed to give readers of this book a 25 percent discount on all digital products; you can go towww.getrefm.com/retitans and use the reference code *retitans*. It is always a good idea to invest in yourself and in expanding your skillset.

Exercise

Pick two properties in your market and find out all you can about them. Practice doing a Back of the Envelop (BOTE) analysis on each one and decide if the opportunities make financial sense. Track them and when they sell, analyze how close you were in your analysis.

Notes

1. https://www.linkedin.com/pulse/principle-51-recognize-1-biggest-threat-good-decision-ray-dalio/.
2. Ray Dalio shared these with CNBC at the World Economic Forum in Davos, Switzerland on January 2018.

Chapter 16

Key Lesson #5: Surround Themselves with Greatness

R eal estate, perhaps more than any other large business, is about people. It's about the connection you can make with other people—between you and the investors, the bankers, the contractors, the architects, and so many other players. You need to be able to communicate with them and understand their needs, incentives, and motivations.

Every person who has ever had any measurable success in real estate has invested time and effort on a consistent basis to connect and develop relationships with other people who are integral parts of the real estate industry. You will interact with brokers, bankers, investors, advisers, market experts, appraisers, builders, architects, interior designers, asset managers, property managers, and others on a regular basis. For example, see the Circles of Influence diagram in Figure 16.1 to get a feel for how a Titan like Gina Diez Barroso spends an average week. She has built relationships with every

CIRCLES OF INFLUENCE

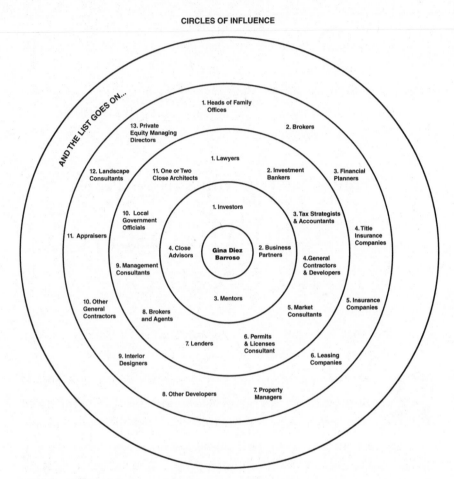

Figure 16.1 People in Gina Diez Barroso's circle of influence.

possible person in the real estate industry. Once you see her reach in the real estate world, you can understand how she can wield such major influence.

The Titans share the humility to know that they are not able to do everything on their own. This is why they surround themselves with great people. Success attracts talent, and exceptional success at the level of these Titans attracts the brightest and the best. People who are committed to becoming winners and doing the work required to succeed want to be associated with other winners. The Titans have learned to be able to deal with people at different skill levels and competencies, but they get to choose the best available talent when they are assembling their own team.[1] That just amplifies the Titan's "impossible is nothing" mindset and further improves their ability to operate successfully.

Surround Yourself with Smarter People

It is easy to understand how Titans can surround themselves with smart people. But how do we do that when we're just starting out? The process begins with understanding your areas of strength. What are your innate talents? What skills have you developed? In which areas of knowledge have focused your studies? What are your current assets? Remember that everyone shares the same and most important asset: time. Ambition and work ethic are also assets. You are fully in control of how you spend or invest your time to pursue your vision and how much effort you are willing to expend to get there. When you are confident about what you bring to the table, you can find people who will be happy to join you, bringing their different resources to support your mission.

Look at your goals and action plan. Make a list of the professionals you need to help you accomplish each one of those goals. Start learning about the professionals in your market. Find out how long they have been in business. Inquire about their involvement in the community and their reputation. Find out if they belong to any networking groups, fraternal organizations, or social clubs. Drop in and introduce yourself and find out what they need from you to help them perform at their peak. That one consideration will automatically put you in higher esteem with them than the average real estate professionals they interact with.

This is how you begin to form alliances and networks. Once you know the people you need to add to your resource list, you will be able to expand your social circle with purpose. Far too many people are part of closed social circles. The 10 or 20 people they know all only know each other. If you are a dentist who only knows other dentists with the same specialty as yours, you may have plenty to talk about, but there isn't much opportunity for you to learn new things.

At an early age, these Titans set their sights on finding and working for the best mentors. Some followed the path that had been forged by their fathers. Others took jobs straight out of college with people who were already doing what they themselves dreamed of doing. They made a conscious choice to listen, observe, take notes, and learn from those who had already learned the hard lessons, worked out an elegant solution, or forged a new path toward profiting in real estate. Making the choice to follow their examples will change the trajectory of your career path above and beyond whatever you may have dared to dream.

Power of the Mastermind

Your first step to surrounding yourself with excellence is to start or join a real estate mastermind. This is a group of people who meet once a week to share what they've been working on, get feedback, and have a chance to gain more wisdom from others. Far too many new real estate entrepreneurs get stuck, operating in isolation and making decisions by themselves. Sometimes, just having someone to listen to your ideas is enough to help you make better decisions.

In addition, a mastermind could become another source of new deals. Because you are surrounding yourself with other people who will want you to succeed, they could pass along opportunities to you. The person in the mastermind might suggest a project they would like to partner on with you; perhaps they can put up most of the capital and you put in the work. Ideally, you'll eventually outgrow that mastermind and look to surround yourself with even bigger players and relationships.

As you look to create relationships, understand your strengths and where you can add value to others. Offer your talent or expertise to people you look up and want to connect with. Offer tips or solutions in areas where these people could possibly use help. Become their friend. A big network with real connections will provide you with more opportunities and you will find that more doors will open.

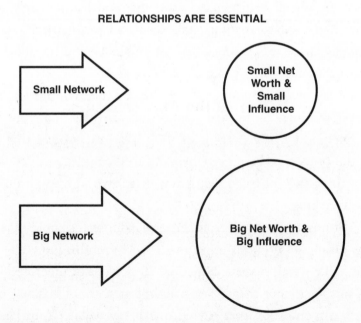

RELATIONSHIPS ARE ESSENTIAL

Small Network

Small Net Worth & Small Influence

Big Network

Big Net Worth & Big Influence

Figure 16.2 A small network can lead to a large network, a big net worth, and notable influence.

Mentors

Finding a great mentor can significantly improve your chances of success because you'll have someone on your side who has already gone through many of the challenges you will likely face. By listening to and learning from someone who has probably already experienced the same problem, you are reducing the probabilities of mistakes you could make. You are also decreasing the time it takes to reach success because you are eliminating the trial-and-error learning method that you would have to use if you were alone.

Good mentors are those who have already achieved success in your chosen field. Good mentors will push you to pursue new challenges and get you out of your comfort zone. They will encourage you to focus on constantly improving and growing. They will identify your weakness, give you constructive feedback, and help you improve. They will help you acknowledge and learn to rely upon your strengths. Good mentors will keep you steady—encouraging you during those tough times that undoubtedly pop up, and keeping you grounded when you make a great deal.

A survey of 200 leading global CEOs by the Stanford Graduate School of Business found that mentorship provides numerous benefits.[2] Specifically, 100 percent of the CEOs mentioned that they enjoy the process of being coached and receiving leadership advice; 78% of the CEOs revealed that it was their own idea to go out and receive coaching.

According to the US Small Business Administration, 30 percent of new businesses do not survive the first 24 months, and 50 percent do not make it past 5 years. However, 70 percent of mentored businesses survive longer than 5 years, and 88 percent of business owners with a mentor say that having one is invaluable.[3] Your chances of success in life and in business can be amplified by having the right mentor.

Good mentors usually have a vast network of people in the same market or industry you are in. They will likely offer to introduce you to new potential investors, developers, business partners, brokers, market consultants, and others.

Both Bob Faith and Ron Terwilliger had Trammel Crow as their mentor. Trammel taught them about hard work, doing things in an ethical way, and thinking big. They took the initiative to learn deeply from his wisdom. You might be wondering how one goes about finding a mentor in the real estate business.

Start with someone you already know. If you are in the real estate business, you can write down a list of people you've met in the business. Further refine your list to individuals you particularly admire. Reach out to them and let them know that you are seeking their advice. Respect their time. If you don't know too many people in the real estate industry you can ask your network for recommendations. Every connection has the potential to open the doors to new connections and opportunities. The very best way to find a mentor, a way that has worked for me, is to focus on giving value first to people that you look up to and aspire to be around.

Giving Value

Giving value means giving something to someone else and expecting nothing in return. The biggest mistake most people make when approaching real estate billionaires or other successful persons in real estate it is to start by asking for something. There is a common misperception that billionaires have everything they need. This is not true. They are also people. But people approach them all the time, asking for things without offering anything in return. It can become tiresome and irritating.

When you are interacting with people you want to connect with, make yourself stand out in the crowd by being the person who sincerely wants to be of service. Leave every conversation knowing more about the other people than they know about you. Be truly interested in the goals of others and ask questions that help them find solutions. You will become an interesting person to them. They will want to talk with you again. Be genuine. Be yourself. People at that top appreciate that far more than you can imagine.

Another way to give value is finding a way to help them with something at which they might not be so proficient. You might meet somebody who is a master at putting together a sophisticated transaction but admittedly clueless when it comes to online marketing and social media. If this is one of your strengths, you can reach out and offer to promote that person's firm or new project on your social media outlets. You could also propose to help train the firm's marketing person in this specific field. Ask for nothing in return.

When you start doing favors without expectation of return for people you deem worthy, something magical happens. You stop getting worried about people returning your favor, and when people start to do favors for you, these will likely be bigger than the favors you did for them. Think of favors as your opportunity to put positive karma and value into the universe and make it a better place. Give from your heart expecting nothing in return. The universe will balance it all out in the end and return to you in much bigger proportions.

Key Takeaways

- Look to surround yourself with outstanding people. Build a resource list of related business professionals in your market and begin to build relationships with them.

- Join a mastermind group or a club filled with people that you look up to. Focus on developing good relationships with people there and learn as much as possible from them.

- Develop situational awareness and always look for ways to give value to others, expecting nothing in return.

- Find a good mentor and learn from that person's experience.

- Become a person who is genuinely interested in help-ing others. You will attract powerful people into your life because you will stand out from the sycophants attracted to success and power.

Exercise

Notice the circles of influence included in this section where I discuss Gina Diez Barroso. I would like you to draw out your circles of influence with the people and companies closest to you in real estate and then expand it outward. By getting a visual image of your current circle of influence, you will get a good idea of how much harder you have to work to reach your goals and objectives. Remember, who you know is very important. Knowing other people who will want you to succeed is essential.

Notes

1. A note on lawyers and tax strategists. As you think about developing your team, you must have at least one lawyer and one tax strategist. Why? Because their professional expertise can save you years of work. When you have major tax or legal issues in real estate, you can quickly lose income that took years to accumulate. However, if you surround yourself with good lawyers and fiscal strategists before making an acquisition, they can save you a lot of time, money, and headaches.

2. Stanford GSB 2013 Executive Coaching Survey.

3. www.sba.gov.

Chapter 17

Key Lesson #6: Extraordinary Salespeople

While we were raising a real estate fund for one of Thor's companies, Thor Urbana, I got to sit in several different meetings with Joe Sitt. Fundraising is all about being a very good salesperson and Joe is one of the great salesmen in real estate. There are several things that you can learn from him. Here are a few of my observations about Joe:

- Joe Sitt is a very charismatic person, always optimistic and often smiling. People like people who smile.
- Joe Sitt is fun and exudes high energy. One of the worst traits a salesperson can have is being boring and low energy.
- Joe Sitt is also an extraordinary storyteller. He has some really exciting stories about the interesting people he surrounds himself with.
- Joe Sitt shows interest when is meeting with other people. He will sit down and listen to you.

I have been in numerous business meetings with Joe and have observed how he interacts with his stakeholders. One of his great strengths is his habit of genuinely praising other people.

Dale Carnegie framed it perfectly: To become a great salesperson, you have to remember that people want to do business with people they like, trust, and respect. How do you get people to like, trust, and respect you? You can start by being sincerely interested in them. This way, you can gain a deeper understanding of these individuals' needs and wants and develop a genuine relationship with them.

I have seen that most people in in real estate forget that enthusiasm carries your message the farthest. Often times, people don't buy into the product or service as much as they buy into the person who is selling it to them. This means that, as a salesperson (every person on earth is a salesperson), it's your job to exude incredible passion for the idea or product you are selling.

Here are seven sales tips that Dale Carnegie recommends:

1. Call people by their name. Learn the names of your prospects. The concept is simple, a person's name, to that person, is the nicest and most important word in the world.

2. Listen. All people want to feel like they are listened to. If you give them a chance to talk to you then you can better understand their needs.

3. Smile. A smile says, "I like you" according to Carnegie. It is hard to not like someone who has a genuine smile.

4. Arouse a desire for customers to buy from you. In other words, create a fear of missing out. Customers will take action to pursue a product or service that they fundamentally want and feel like they are being left out of. One way to create this is using the principle of scarcity.

5. Avoid arguments. This may seem like common sense, but it is not common practice. I have seen so many people in the real estate industry who engage in arguments with potential buyers, partners, and investors. Do not argue or criticize.

6. Put yourself in the customer's shoes and show genuine interest in the other person. Customers need to know how the product or service you are selling will benefit them.

7. Use showmanship to sell your ideas. Carnegie tells the story of a salesman marketing cash registers who told a grocer that the registers his store was using were so old that he was throwing money away, literally. After saying this, the salesman threw several coins on the floor to show what he meant. He got the sale. There are many other subtle examples like this one that you could use.

Sell the Dream

All the successful people I have ever met in real estate—and business—are very good salespersons. They have mastered key skills in the underlying psychology of the sales process. These include building rapport with a potential client, usually by giving the client something while expecting nothing in return. This could be a piece of information or something as simple as offering a bottle of water or a cup of coffee. Good salespersons put people at ease and lay the foundation for gaining their trust. Once people feel at ease with you, they are more receptive to the fact that you are a knowledgeable authority in your field and you have expertise in the subject being discussed. You are consistent in that your actions match your words.

Many people today seem to believe the word "selling" implies misleading, coaxing, stressing, or in some way manipulating someone into making a purchasing decision. On the contrary, you should think of selling as a logical part of explaining the benefits to be reaped once the purchasing decision has been made. Sales skills are needed to convince investors, partners, lenders, and other stakeholders that a specific real estate development or investment will generate an attractive return for them. These skills will also help you source deals, land new partners, negotiate better prices, increase rents, decrease expenses, and much more.

Fundamentally, having good sales skills means having good communications skills. Real estate is a people business; therefore, communication skills are critical.

If you sit down with Bob Faith you will quickly learn that he is a great communicator. He is genuine with his clients and investors. He is amicable. He is optimistic. He is assertive. He is a problem solver. During his early years he would have to fill the role of property manager on several of his buildings. The tenants always had dozens of excuses for why they were reluctant to pay him rent. He was always able to convince them that they were getting great value for what they were paying.

During one of our conversations, Bob said that one great skill a person can acquire in life is to sit down across the table from someone else and get that person to agree to do something. That's true whether you are trying to get a 1000-square-foot lease signed or whether you are closing a $2 billion transaction. One of the main things is how you position yourself in a way that makes sense to the other person; that is the critical part of any negotiation.

When I was first starting off my career one of my mentors told me that in business "the person with the most certainty will almost always win the negotiation or sale." I have certainly seen this to be the case in my life. Throughout my career I have been involved in large real estate closings, in public roadshow meetings, in raising a public investment vehicle, and in other high-stakes transactions. In many cases groups with very good ideas were not successful in achieving their goals. Why? Because they did not know how to sell their company and investment thesis. They might have been the smartest people in the room, but they were not good enough at sales.

For example, no matter in what part of the real estate industry you are in, after a few days you will start hearing hear the word "no" quite often. No matter, you have to keep going. The difference between a Titan and an average person is that the Titan sees "no" as a fun challenge and not as a rejection, because most Titans do not understand what the word "no" means. One Titan told me that it was an acronym for "Not Over." Titans might give up after hearing "no" a dozen times(maybe years after), and only if said emphatically. They certainly won't give up after the first few rejections.

A Surprising Fact About Sales

Becoming an extraordinary salesperson is a learned trait. Some may be naturally gifted at relating to people and feel comfortable sharing with them. Some may truly believe that they are doing a great service or responding to a higher calling. The truth is that people are often rewarded in public for what they practice for years in private.

One of my biggest takeaways from interviewing the Titans is that really great salespersons are actually not those who are loud and extroverted but those who are deft at switching between introverted and extroverted behaviors, flexing as needed.

Many of the Titans change their approach to fit the situation in order to make the other person feel more comfortable and to best accomplish their goal. By doing this, they are much more likely to be successful in influencing others.

Erika Andersen, author and founder of the consulting, coaching, and training company Proteus International, shares the following three tips on becoming versatile.[1]

1. **Observe first:** When you first meet someone (especially someone who's important to your success), note how they behave. Are they loud or soft? Fast-paced or slower? Immediately friendly or more reserved?

2. **"Move" toward them:** If some of your habitual behaviors are very different from those you observe, try shifting them as you interact with this person. For instance, if he or she is fast-paced and loud, and you tend to be more soft-spoken and quieter, try speaking up and speeding up a little. If this other person is more formal and reserved, while you're naturally more friendly and informal—try holding back a little on the friendliness; be willing to engage on a level of formality that the other person uses.

3. **Don't confuse how you act with who you are:** Some people resist trying this kind of "flexing" because they fear it will be unnatural or inauthentic. Please understand—I'm not encouraging you to change your beliefs or values, or to say anything untrue: Versatility is simply shifting your behaviors. Think of it this way: If you were conversing with someone from France who knew very little English, and you spoke pretty good French—would you insist on speaking English with this person because it was more comfortable for you? Would you feel you were somehow compromising your integrity if you spoke French?

If you make it a habit to take this approach when meeting new people, you'll be in that sweet spot of interpersonal flexibility where great salespeople—and great managers and leaders—live and thrive.

A Sales Master at WeWork

Adam Neumann is one of the most extraordinary salespeople I have ever met.[2] In 2010, he innovated—and revolutionized—the concept of the office space when he co-founded the communal workspace giant WeWork.

The business model might appear to be relatively simple: WeWork rents office space from landlords in wholesale, breaks the space into smaller units, and creates a flexible, nontraditional work environment that provides a fun experience for all, and subleases it at a profit to its final users.

Adam explains that WeWork is not really a real estate company; it's a state of consciousness with a generation of interconnected emotionally intelligent entrepreneurs. A state of consciousness? Adam Neumann believes in this idea, and is therefore successful in selling this mindset to his investors. In large part, his sales skills are what allow him to raise money at such spectacular valuations.

As I am writing this book, WeWork is raising money at a $45 billion valuation, which tops the market caps of some of the largest REITs in the world like Public Storage and Prologis. Keep in mind that WeWork had total revenue of $886 million but a net loss of $933 million in 2017. In order to raise money at a $45 billion valuation for a company in the real estate business that had net losses of almost a billion dollars the year before means that you have to be a grandiose seller of your ideas.

Here is one of many stories about Adams sales skills. A few years ago, the union that represents property service workers in New York protested outside WeWork locations because many of their contracted nonunion workers were making $10 an hour.

Adam sat down with Héctor Figueroa, president of the 32BJ Service Employees International Union. Figueroa said after the meeting that he met with Adam to talk about the employees, but they ended up having a conversation "about who we are as people." The two came to an agreement by which Adam hired back some of the now unionized workers at $18.46 an hour and gave them health benefits.

At the end of the negotiation, Figueroa gave Neumann a union jacket, only the second time in his 17 years as a union officer that he remembers extending this gesture toward an employer.

Adam Neumann is prodigious at selling because he is very effective at sharing his vision and he is passionate about what he is selling. He also has a great deal of professional equity that he has built up over the years. He has a good reputation. He has relationships that span the full spectrum of real estate, from banking to construction to marketing, all of which allow him to have access to answers about any issue that is likely to come up in any transaction. Adam is educated, smart, and experienced. People do business with Adam because they trust, like, and respect him.

Presentation Skills

It is critical to your success in the real estate industry that you are able to communicate. It is not uncommon for a real estate professional to be asked to make a presentation before a board of directors, a planning and zoning commission, or a homeowner's association. The confidence, sincerity, and clarity with which you present your project will often decide whether it gets rejected, delayed until more questions are answered, or gains unanimous approval to move forward.

You can observe others giving presentations to see communication skills in action. There are books and online courses that will teach you the basic skills as well. The majority of those who are experts at giving presentations will tell you that the best way to learn how to make effective presentations is to do it and get objective feedback on areas where you need improvement. One of the best ways to do that is join a Toastmasters club.

Toastmasters International is "a non-profit educational organization that teaches public speaking and leadership skills through a worldwide network of clubs."[3] Ralph Smedley developed the program in 1905, and the first official Toastmasters club began in 1924. There are now over more than 357,000 members in more than 16,600 clubs in 143 different countries. While there are slight variations in format, every Toastmasters club is dedicated to providing a supportive and positive learning experience in which members are empowered to develop communication and leadership skills, resulting in greater self-confidence and personal growth. There is a nominal membership fee, but the value gained far exceeds the investment. Not only do you follow a time-tested experiential process as you learn to become a polished speaker, you also learn leadership skills and develop a network of supportive people from a wide variety of backgrounds and professions.

Key Takeaways

- People want to do business with people they like, trust, and respect. One way to get people to like you is by being genuinely interested in them.
- Becoming an extraordinary salesperson is a learned trait.
- Fundamentally, having good sales skills means having good communications skills.

Exercise

- Read the book, *How to Win Friends & Influence People* by Dale Carnegie.
- Locate a Toastmasters International club near you (https://www.toastmasters.org/find-a-club) and join it. Complete the Competent Communicator program.

Notes

1. Anderson's advice appeared in Forbes: https://www.forbes.com/sites/erikaandersen/2013/04/12/the-unexpected-secret-to-being-a-great-salesperson/#772e8d584455; see Proteus website at www.proteus-international.com.

2. Please note that Adam Neumann was not interviewed but I include him in the book because he is one of best salespeople I have ever seen. I had the pleasure of meeting him and doing business with WeWork.

3. https://www.toastmasters.org/about.

Chapter 18

Key Lesson #7: Execute their Ideas

Throughout most of my life teachers and elders have told me that knowledge is power. I do not believe that knowledge is power—I believe it is only potential power. True power lies in execution. You must be able to execute—a deal, a plan, a goal, or a solution. Your dream opportunity to gain a taste of success will only become possible if you are able to execute.

Analysis Paralysis

Many real estate investors freeze at some point in their journey because they get caught in overanalysis or get scared to take the next step. They feel unsure and unable to make a decision because they think they need more information. I can understand that because most of us have been there at some point. Urs Ledermann addresses that uncertainty by being mindful, aware of our options, and being present in the moment.

The only way through this impasse is to act. Think about any example from sports. There comes a moment when a professional ski racer is standing in the starting gate and must stop analyzing the course ahead and push out of the starting gate or be disqualified. A professional basketball player has a split second when a teammate is open under the basket and the time is right to pass the ball to get the score. In soccer, a midfielder catches a momentary glance of the striker catching the last defender too far upfield and must execute a pass before the ref calls "offsides."

Each one of these moments of execution comes after countless hours of training, preparation, and repetitively practicing the moment in one's mind so that when the opportunity presents itself, the athlete can execute the required physical action. It is the same in real estate.

Sometimes we all get caught up in the belief that if we just have one more piece of critical information, we can make the right decision. This is where we have to exercise emotional maturity. There is no such thing as perfection. It is an abstract concept and a fool's errand to think that someday we will be able to put together the "perfect deal." As Richard Ziman pointed out, our goal should be to put together a lot of good deals and not have too many bad deals. Just keep it in perspective. An occasional deal will come along to every real estate professional that makes us wish we had made different choices. It seems to be part of this process. That is when a Titan remembers that without risk, there can be no reward.

Richard Mack gave one of the best illustrations about execution as being the result of anticipation. Wayne Gretzky, one of the greatest hockey players of all time, said what made him great is that he skates to where the puck is going to be, not where it currently is. It's the power of anticipating. I apply this in real estate to mean that you must anticipate, as best you can, most of the challenges that will arise once you execute. Be ready for these risks.

Ziman laid out his template for helping to mitigate execution risk. His success factors are timing, location, debt timing, and understanding demand. Buying a property at the right time determines how much value you can add and when you can sell it for the optimal profit. At a minimum, you want a location that meets the minimum requirements for the asset class of the property in areas including but not limited to market value, access, supporting infrastructure, environmental integrity, statutory compliance, and market demand. How much equity is available? Is financing available? Finally, have you determined your market and the amount of existing demand for what you are offering?

There's a certain point where we have enough information to make an educated decision, even though we don't have absolute knowledge. We will never reach this point because no one knows what the future holds, and there is no such thing as perfection.

"It's not your ability to predict what will come next that guarantees success," says Elie Horn. "It's your ability to adapt when it comes."

One of the first questions you must address is how you are going to mitigate the various risks. Remember that most of the Titans focused on this concept, trying to understand the downsides. There are the macro questions: Where are interest rates now? Is it likely that they will go up? Is inflation stable or will it likely increase? Is consumer confidence high? Is the economy growing or is it headed toward a recession?

Then there are more specific questions that have to do with the local economy, such as a major retail chain with a store in the local market filing for bankruptcy, or the local municipality imposing higher taxes on new real estate development. Or what if your city has a boom in construction and the demand for materials and construction machines has significantly increased, adversely affecting your budget?

These could all be important considerations if you are considering purchasing a grocery-anchored neighborhood shopping center and your supermarket anchor has just announced that it is moving to a newer location. Perhaps the local municipality has decided that there is too much new development going on and the infrastructure (roads, public transportation, hospitals, public schools, etc.) are currently not adequate to attend all this new demand. Road construction can have a significant impact on the monthly earnings of a retail shopping center.

Or imagine if the price of steel suddenly increased by 30 percent due to supply constraints. You might want to rethink your plans for building a high-rise mixed-use building.

There are many questions that must be answered about the location and desirability of the property. Are the neighboring properties supportive of your vision for the investment? Are there environmental issues? What kind of access is there to the property? Does the asset have good frontage to a main avenue? Is there adequate utility infrastructure such as water supply and sewer to support construction on that site?

A fundamental element of the real estate profession is timing. If you spend months trying to find the perfect piece of information, by the time you make your decision, that information is likely to no longer be relevant. You can end up in an endless cycle of constantly needing new information because half of the information you're using to make your decision has now expired. You lost the opportunity.

"The average person thinks real estate is just about knowledge," said Carlos Betancourt. "[It's] just about hitting the books and learning about cap rates, and then you can start making a lot of money."

The truth is that success in the real estate profession often boils down to the conclusions you draw after you have analyzed and digested all of the data.

As Carlos Betancourt pointed out, even if you are surrounded by extremely smart people from very prestigious schools and top companies, people who have higher IQs than you do, or elaborate financial models, they can nevertheless miss the big picture because they're too focused on the math, the numbers, and the little details.

When you have that narrow mindset, you get tunnel vision, and you begin to major in minors. You must have the comprehensive vision of the Titan mindset. When you have reached the point where you are the closest to maximum knowledge without hitting the point of diminishing returns, you are at the point where you should decide. The more experience you gain, the more you will learn to identify this point.

Let's use an example and say you are looking at an existing multifamily building; it's been in operation for 20 years, but it's in a very good location that continues to grow and show strong demand.

Here are some basic, important issues to consider: How far away is it from the local coffee shop? From a gym? From local transportation such as buses and metro stations? From the central business districts? What socioeconomic level surrounds your property? What do the demographics look like?

Because the property is 20 years old, you will likely want to be able to do a manageable amount of updating and upgrading to maximize the appreciation. If you are looking to obtain acquisition financing, one of the first things you need to do is calculate whether the net income from the rents will be sufficient to cover the debt service.

How about capital expenditures? (This will also be a requirement if the building has been in operation for only a few years.) What is the physical condition of the property at closing? What will be the costs of refreshing the grounds, updating the common areas, repairing the mechanical and electrical systems, updating the HVAC system, and others?

If you have rental properties, you have to handle leasing and you need to arrange for property management. Which experienced company will help you with the leasing? If you have institutional investors you also have to consider asset management. Do you have the expertise to lease and manage your property? Do you have the time?

Bottom-line thinking is also required. What kind of profit will this investment yield? Will it be a deal that will help you create a good track record? Does it make sense with your overall strategy? Are parts of the process duplicable for future deals? Can you realize economies of scale or scope? Is this project the best available investment of your resources at this time? These are all important questions that you should be able to answer in order to execute. Remember that there are multiple paths up the mountain.

Let's analyze a real-world example that a friend shared with me. (To protect his privacy I've called him Wang Wei. I've also changed the numbers and reduced the amount of deal information to simplify the analysis.) Wang Wei is the Chief Investment Officer for a Real Estate Titan in China. Wang gets a call one day from a trusted friend of his—I'll call him Mike—who works at CBRE, a leading global real estate brokerage firm.

Mike is approaching Wang Wei to sell him a 400,000-square-foot warehouse/logistical center in Pudong, an important industrial district within greater Shanghai. The asking price is $20 million, but Wang Wei knows that asking prices can be negotiated; the owner is motivated to sell the asset to pay off debt to the bank.

Mike mentions that the property has three different tenants and recommends making some capital expenditure improvements to the building to slowly raise the rents in the coming months. The occupancy in the Pudong district is very high at 97 percent. There is currently almost no construction going on, but there are several plots of land still available in the district. This is not great news because it means the barriers to entry are not as high as you'd want them to be.

The asking price of the asset is $50 per square foot. Because Wang Wei works for a firm that owns other similar properties within this market, he knows that it costs between $50 and $53 per square foot to develop a comparable logistics center in the area. That includes the cost of the land, permits and licenses, architecture and engineering, all construction, leasing and development fees, financing, and all else involved with development.

Wang Wei knows that buying existing real estate at or below replacement cost, in a strong market (where demand exceeds supply) within a good location makes sense.

Mike further explains to Wang Wei that the current net operating income of the property is $2.2 million, which would represent a going-in cap rate (or yield) of 11 percent. They both know that other comparable properties on the Pudong market have traded at between 8 and 9 percent cap rates, so there is a 200 to 300 basis point spread between what they would be paying and the most recent market comps.

The pros and cons are given in Table 18.1.

Because Wang Wei knows the market and has already been involved in numerous industrial transactions in Shanghai, he knows that this

Table 18.1   Pros and Cons of Purchasing a Warehouse in Pudong

PROS	CONS
Good location in high demand market	Only 3 tenants in place
Well designed with high quality construction	Large empty land plots nearby (risk of future competition)
Only 7-year-old building	Capital expenditures are needed
Good access to public transportation	Streets need resurfacing
Credit-worthy tenants in place	
Acquire asset at or below replacement cost	
Leases expire in 6 years	
Attractive returns	
Motivated seller (good probability of closing)	

is an attractive opportunity that offers above market returns with minimum risk. Therefore, after the call and reviewing the offering memorandum, Wang Wei thinks that this potential acquisition deserves serious attention.

The same day he gets the call, Wang Wei makes an appointment to visit the property the following day with his boss. (Please note that you should never consider buying a property before walking it—and the market—at least once, ideally a few times.)

After the site visit they see that everything is in place and they decide to schedule a meeting with the seller. Wang Wei prepares a Letter of Intent offering to pay the asking price.

(The reason he chooses not to negotiate the price is to ask for a 30-day exclusivity and quickly remove all competitors from the transaction. Experienced real estate players understand that when a very attractive deal presents itself, speed becomes very important and therefore many times they choose to focus on removing competitors instead of negotiating.)

They succeed in signing the letter of intent and perform a due diligence on the property to make sure they are comfortable acquiring the asset.

The story is meant to provide an example of a property opportunity where the buyers gathered enough information after only a few days. However, this is in part because they are experienced players who know the market they are investing in very well.

Timing

The interviews with the Titans also highlighted the importance of timing when executing.

Specifically, there are two very important points in the execution stage: when you buy and when you sell. Buying the right project from the right customer at the right time in the cycle can save you years of hard work and many basis points on your returns. In the same way, selling the right project to the right buyer at the right time in the cycle can have the same effect. It is therefore important to remember that you should be buying when most are not and not buying when most are. In other words, you should be a contrarian investor. As you think about buying or selling, try as best as you can to understand the data and speak with people that have a good notion of which point in the cycle you could be in.

Belief in Yourself

Once you have all the necessary information there is another thing that you need to deal with, your mindset (remember Lesson #1). Many people, even when they have the very best information, sometimes decide that it is better not to execute. Many Titans believe that it is better to give up on a potentially good deal than it is to execute a bad one. That is most certainly true. However, at some point you have to believe in yourself, mitigate as many risks as you can, and act.

Allow me to illustrate the concept with an allegory. Imagine you are sailing in the Caribbean with a friend and suddenly, the engines of the boat stop functioning. You have struck a piece of floating wreckage that has knocked off both propellers and damaged the hull. Seawater has flooded the engine compartment and knocked out all electronics on board. You have no radio, you are out of cell phone range, and you cannot get an internet signal.

You also have no water or food left on the boat. Your charts show that you are not in any regular shipping lanes, but there is an island about eight miles away from your last known location. You are slowly drifting toward the island, but you calculate it will be 14 to 16 hours before you even get close. You know, however, that on the island there are people living and you can get internet and cell service.

As darkness falls, you decide to shoot off a signal flare, hoping that someone spots it and comes to rescue you. Two hours later, you shoot up another signal flare, but nobody comes. You decide to save your last flare for an emergency. You and your friend decide to get some sleep, taking rotating shifts so that someone is always on the lookout for a light coming from the dark, empty sea.

Dawn breaks and you calculate that that the island is still eight miles away. You decide that the best course of action is to swim to get help. The boat is drifting at a rate of about one-half mile per hour. You know from experience that you can swim a mile in calm seas in about an hour.

You begin studying the waters, don a life vest, get an extra life vest, strap a compass to your wrist, and dive in. Four hours later, much sooner than expected, you get to the island! Yes, there could have been sharks or jellyfish. Yes, you could have miscalculated your direction and missed the island; but none of that happened. You weighed the risks and took action. Failure was simply not an option. You had to execute to reap the upside. It is the same in real estate; you need to execute to get the potential rewards. In other words, you need to jump in the water.

It takes a person with self-confidence and belief to think about attempting such a feat. As human beings, we are often able to summon a previously unknown reservoir of courage and strength when faced with hardship. I am not suggesting that real estate investment is a life-or-death situation, but all Titans at some point in their careers had to face the prospect of massive failures, and that self-belief and determination got them through those times. Failure was not an option.

Final Thoughts

As you noticed in the interviews and lessons, there are a variety of ways and routes for people to start a career in real estate and get the top. The Titans come from different geographies, backgrounds, and ethnicities, and they have very different levels of education. Real estate is an entrepreneurial field and you therefore play an important role in your own success.

The real estate industry provides you with the opportunity to do things that will have a positive and wonderful impact on the world. You will be able to create jobs, design beautiful buildings, improve the quality of life for final users, and so much more.

If you are now ready to take your place in the real estate industry, or grow your place within the business, and you implement these 7 key lessons, you will see the value of your real estate business take off in a matter of months. The growth will be like nothing you've ever experienced.

Remember what Napoleon Hill said: "Whatever the mind can conceive and believe, the mind can achieve."

Greatness awaits you.

Appendix A:
A Conversation with Wharton's Dr. Peter Linneman

This book would not be complete without including the most renowned real estate professor in the world, Peter Linneman, who pioneered the academic study of real estate and was named by the National Association of Realtors as one of the 25 most influential people in the business. I have so much respect for him not only because he did the research on real estate for decades, but also because he executed as a professional and carried out large investments and dispositions. In the real estate industry there are so many people that you encounter who express their opinions as if they were truths, and I am not a fan of this practice. I believe that opinions should be based on facts. Peter Linneman makes shrewd conclusions based on research, on evidence, and real-world facts. So, of course, do the Titans interviewed in this book.

In His Own Words

I wasn't born into real estate, and it certainly wasn't something that I grew up expecting to become a part of my life. I stumbled into it through the world of finance. Earlier in my career, I was working leveraged buyouts (LBOs) at Wharton, which is where you buy out a company by making use of debt.

When you're in the LBO world, the expectation is that the return generated on the acquisition will more than outweigh the interests that you have to pay on the debt, making it a good way to experience high returns while only risking a small amount of capital.

The Dean of Wharton at the time asked me to create a real estate curriculum at the school.

I didn't know much about real estate and I was probably a little bored at the time with what I was doing at the university. Therefore, I accepted and said, "Okay, let's put together an advisory board of Al Taubman and a bunch of other leaders from different parts of the real estate industry."

In the process, I started to learn about real estate from Al Taubman, who became an amazing friend and teacher.

Taubman is most well known for being the father of the modern shopping center and for owning Sotheby's.

I learned a great deal from him, and together, we created a program that we call "System." I slowly moved toward real estate assignments, and instead of doing buyouts for paper bag companies or whatever, I would focus on doing it for a real estate company.

At the time, real estate was all about details and not a truly professional business.

Ultimately, I ended up in the real estate industry, and it was a time when you were able to leverage an unbelievable 93 percent. We would put up 7 percent of the value in cash and the other 93 percent was debt.

With the collapse of the late 1980s and early 1990s, you had millionaires and billionaires who had no idea what was on their balance sheets. They didn't know what an income statement was, as crazy as that sounds.

I rose through the real estate ranks because I understood both classroom and real-world business. Since the early 1990s, real estate has changed dramatically. Now you've got public companies and private equity firms, and because of my background evaluating companies, I knew which ones were good bets and which ones weren't.

Real Estate Deals

My first deal was a condo for my family. I was renting, but I wanted to mess with the place, knock down walls, and build it like a home. We wanted to double the size of the apartment. It's hard to find two adjacent owners who will let you tear things up like that.

We bought two adjacent units and we got it right. It's hard to find a unit that's big where we were living. We bought because it gave us control, not because I thought it was an exceptional investment.

My first large transaction, however, was the Rockefeller Center in New York in 1994 and 1995. There was a foreclosure because the Japanese owners during the early to mid 1990s were trying to restructure and sell off the building.

I was chairman of a public company, so I wound up as chairman of the company that owned that particular debt. I was lucky to have an excellent board with people like Peter Pearson, who was one of the co-founders of Blackstone, and Benjamin Holloway, who was chairman of Equitable, the second largest insurance company in United States. A couple of other amazing people were also on the board and one of the lead partners of Goldman Sachs as well.

I learned so much in that process. It was pretty successful in the end, and in an odd way, I learned that the smart guys really are smart.

Personally, I've never been a "deal person." My main contribution over the years has always been one of two things. First it's on the education side, including my publication of a book and developing a program in teaching; this has been a big part of the professionalization of real estate industry over the last 30 years. My second major contribution is that I helped a lot of people think through their business strategy analytically, and I provided an intellectual framework and vocabulary they could use to make their own deals.

Looking back on my deals, my favorite one is the Rockefeller Center deal. Another was in Europe, for a public company called Atrium European Real Estate. It was a complex situation, and everyone was at each other's throats. The company was getting liquidated and there were several institutional investors involved.

I led a restructuring on behalf of the other shareholders, so you can imagine how many people wanted a piece. It took about a year and two different negotiations to get it resolved.

One of my companies is called American Land Fund. My main lesson, as a result of owning this business, is that timing is everything, and you don't control the timing. We felt the housing market was going down. We thought land would be available at distressed prices. We thought we would get a perfect entitlement during the down phase because we would have capital and then, as things recovered, we would sell into the recovery.

We were right about the distress occurring. We were right that there would be distressed opportunities. We were right that we could add amenities that would add value during the down period, but we were wrong about the depth of the job, which was twice as deep as I predicted.

I thought we'd only be in a recession for three to four years, but things still aren't back to normal, and you can't do anything to make somebody buy your land.

If nobody wants to build houses, it's because nobody wants to buy them, and it doesn't matter how cheap your land is.

Compare selling land with owning an apartment. If you own an apartment, you can cut the rent. You can be aggressive because people have to live somewhere. Eventually, someone will show up, but with land, someone has to come and build on the land. That's a second investment. It's a tough asset in that way, and timing is everything in the land business.

It's taken me a decade to do what I thought would take three years, and you can do the math on that. Some people ask me whether they should leverage their own deals when investing in land. My advice is no; in land you should leverage as little as possible, with a maximum of 30 percent.

When you're buying raw land, the value of homes going up or down will affect the value of the land as well. If home prices are going down, the value of your land goes down, and if prices go up, you're lucky enough that your land price goes up. That's enough leverage and risk to have in the deal.

You don't need to add a second layer to that leverage because when you do, that's a recipe for disaster.

Unfortunately, so many of our peers get greedy and take on a lot of debt in order to get their hands on a lot of land. When it takes longer than expected to flip that land, then they get wiped out of their investment.

We were patient and used cash rather than leverage, so we're still standing now.

I know everybody isn't into doing massive deals like that. A lot of people are regular guys working 9 to 5, and they should implement a diverse strategy.

If you can scrape together a little money to put into real estate, you might be better off buying some REITs. For example, $10 worth of assignment, $10 worth of equity residential, $10 worth of regency, and $10 worth of a nitty gritty supply-chain company like Prologis. Why? That's because they're really well managed. They're good portfolios. They're highly diversified, and you get a nice return. I trust these REITs a lot more than development groups.

On the other hand, if you're looking to have a long-term career, my view is that you should start by working for the one of the bigger companies just so you can get some experience around people who know what they're doing: companies like Related, Blackstone, Starwood, Simon, and others. You don't have to work for a household name, but you want a big, stable brand with managers who know what they're doing.

I suggest that for three reasons. One, it's better to lose someone else's money than to go out and invest your own. When you start out, you're going to make mistakes, and people will avoid you. You're going to lose your own money if you start out that way. But if you work for a big company, there are other people who already made those mistakes, and they will stop you from doing the same. You'll learn the reason why it's not good to do that.

Second, it's great to see how a successful firm operates, and the third thing is that you'll see what big firms do. Big firms are big because they do certain things excellently, and these things allow them to scale. By working for those big firms, you'll see what they do so well, and then you can focus on those areas of excellence. If you're entrepreneurial, or you want to work with a smaller firm, seeing what the big firms will still allow you, with your smaller entrepreneurial firm, to avoid the things they do poorly and take advantage of the things they do well.

The Next Generation

What if you're a young person trying to get involved in real estate?

If you've ever seen one of those movies where the guy takes apart his machine gun and then puts it back together wearing a blindfold, that should be how you run and operate Excel. You should become a spreadsheet master because the better you are with Excel and understanding numbers, the better you'll be in this business. Learn how to make it look good and presentable, so you can build a model that someone else can look at and immediately understand.

Bosses don't want to do these financial models themselves. It's an inefficient use of their time, and this is a great way for you to get your foot in the door. The other skill is to read, study, listen, and master your trade. Read about the markets, supply, and things that cause demand. Understand who the major players are, even if you're not in a public company. How much of their success is just riding momentum, or are they doing something really different? Is it bullshit "PR" value-add, or is it real? If you're in town, look at the market. Who's renting what? Why?

Become an expert on your region and the part of the market you're focusing on. Depth of knowledge is always superior to breadth of knowledge. Everywhere you go, there is an opportunity to pay attention to real estate. If you're heading to a building for a meeting, look around and ask, why is the lobby like this? How could they have made the floor plan better? What materials did they use for the construction? Why are the ceilings a certain height?

Be intellectually curious and think about the way different pieces of real estate are tied together.

If you're interested in warehouses, make sure that you study what's happening in retail, because the retail businesses in your area affect what's happening in warehouses and parts of the industrial sector. Most of the stuff you read in the newspapers is not 100 percent true. Most newspaper articles were written to draw attention and attract readers rather than to inform.

In addition to taking newspaper articles with a grain of salt, I recommend that you have good taste in choosing who you decide to work with for the first five to seven years of your career. Make sure you work for a good teacher, and I don't mean you should choose from among university professors. I mean you should choose people who pass on their knowledge and feed their wisdom to you. They can be mentors even if nobody's ever heard of them.

Some people are just instinctively good teachers. They share what they're doing, they share their questions and their answers, and they share their own experiences. Be open to learning and work for somewhere who has the same values as you do.

If you value long-term relationships, don't choose a high turnover company. Find a company that matches your belief, your family's schedule, and your lifestyle.

As much as these ideas are important, the most critical element is mindset, which begins with intellectual curiosity.

Across the board, the most successful people I know read a lot. They're always looking for new knowledge and new information. Each of them excels in a different way. They have different areas of excellence, both in how they interpret data and analyze real estate sectors in the regions where they invest. But one thing they have in common is possessing excellent skills for analyzing something.

The ability to analyze is what creates greatness. Success in this business is always data-driven.

Bad Partners

One common mistake I made was to partner on a deal even though I knew the partners weren't up to their part of the bargain. I knew they didn't have the capital. I knew they didn't have the bandwidth. I knew in my heart of hearts that they didn't have the expertise.

I knew it, so why did I do the deal?

Part of it is that you decide to give potential partners an opportunity—you reach out a hand to bring them up to your level and partner with them—but it ends in tears, and this especially happens when you have employees. You promote people because they've done a great job at their level, and you want to give them the opportunity to move up to the next level. You want to give them a chance to grow and show that they're capable of that next level, but it turns out they're not. This is where the phrase "people are promoted to the level of their incompetence" comes from.

There are other big mistakes in real estate, like over-leveraging. Those are big mistakes, but with leveraging, it's really about a risk assessment. When the mistakes involve employees or partners, it's often because you trust somebody that you shouldn't be. That's a much more personal mistake.

Heroes

One of my biggest heroes is Lucille Ford, a woman who is 96 years old as I am writing this book. If she lived in New York instead of Ohio, she would be a legend, and everyone would know her name.

She received an MBA from Northwestern in 1946, at a time when women did not get MBAs. She ran her family business, then sold it, got a PhD in economics, started teaching, and eventually became a dean at Ashland University.

I've learned more from her than anybody about how to ask yourself hard questions and how to live a quality life. She's living proof that you can become something beyond what anyone might expect. I needed that inspiration as I moved through my career.

I also had the blessing of being a student of Milton Friedman. As one of the three top economists of the 1900s, he taught the "markets over mandarins" theory; he was my professor at University of Chicago, and a close friend for years after.

My third mentor was Al Taubman, who was a giant of real estate, the father of the modern shopping center, and a person of quality. He didn't just teach me real estate; he taught me how to do business.

Lessons

One of the lessons I'd like for you to take away, and this is something that I learned from the book *The Rational Optimist* by Nicholas Redley, is that we should try to be loved, to love, and to be productive.

As much as I'm excited about this book and the way you're going to learn from all these principles, I hope you will always remember what it felt like when you were starting out, so that you can be in alignment with people.

Make the world a better place and make sure that you are remembered as a great real estate person, not a villain.

Appendix B:
Value Add—A Case
Study

I hope that throughout this book it has become clear that one of the best investment strategies in real estate is the value-add approach. Value-add opportunities exist everywhere, even more so in advanced economies like the United States or the United Kingdom. You can come across them by walking or driving through neighborhoods, speaking with brokers and friends in the real estate industry, checking listings online, and using other methods. They basically consist of repositioning a property by improving the operational strategy—that could mean increasing occupancy, lowering operational expenses, increasing rents to market (in case they are lower than market), creating new income streams from unused spaces, and more. The asset will be worth more when you manage to increase the net operating income (NOI). In some cases, a value-add approach can also be a focus on purchasing poorly leased properties in good locations, or properties that have substantial near-term lease rollover. An important metric when you implement this strategy is to be cognizant that you are buying at a similar price (or below) replacement cost.

When you take the value-add approach you take on some risks; however, you don't have to deal with the permits and licenses risk or the construction risks, two significant risks, especially for someone with only a few years of real estate experience. The "construction" risk in value-add is usually associated with light renovations, such as capital improvements (i.e. new walls and a terrace), certain structural repairs, painting several parts of the building, and so on. When you surround yourself with experienced professionals and incentivize them correctly, these risks are very manageable.

Case Study—Altavista 147 in Mexico City, Mexico

Investment Thesis

Thor Urbana, a large real estate development firm, identified a specialty retail center on a high street in southern Mexico City that had little foot traffic and a unique upside potential. The owners at Thor Urbana walked the neighborhood, the street, and the property and

Figure A2.1   Altavista 147

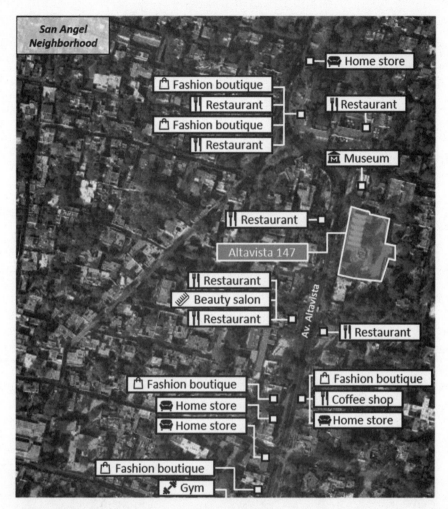

Figure A2.2 Retail space around Altavista 147.

noticed that although the property was 90 percent leased, there was unrealized upside potential. The property was not efficiently designed, it had unused spaces that could generate income, little foot traffic, and the center only had luxury tenants (they might be great tenants, but they bring in little foot traffic).

Thor Urbana approached the seller, developed a friendly relationship, and quickly negotiated to take it off the market. The company performed a thorough due diligence, during which time its vast network with retailers—and its operating experience—enabled it to create a repositioning strategy for the asset.

After acquiring the asset, Thor's strategy consisted of:

- Renovating leases with selected tenants (Thor checked that they were paying below market rents) and bringing up the rents to market. This took time and negotiation skills.
- Removing the low energy tenants bringing little traffic to the center. Instead, it integrated renowned food and beverage outlets and a specialized fitness center that increased the operation hours of the retail center (long operations can mean more sales) and increased traffic.
- Redesigning the leasable space to maximize it without compromising the unique and differentiated experience offered to customers.
- Removing inefficiencies in the operations by previous owners and decreasing operating and maintenance costs of the project without decreasing the quality and service level of the property.
- Hiring a new parking operator to provide better customer service to final users.
- Increasing Gross Leasable Area by 33 percent with a minimal investment.

Investment Outcome

The results were as follows:

Total sales of tenants grew over 40 percent in a three-year period. As of November 2018, and after the implementation of Thor's repositioning strategy, the asset has seen a + 300 percent NOI growth in three years in what was considered an already stabilized asset with a + 90 percent occupancy at the time of acquisition.

Realized Returns

	Underwriting	Current Performance
Levered IRR	17.4%	40.5%
Yield on Cost	10.0%	16.3%

Glossary

Below are some important terms that every person in the myriad fields of real estate should know; however, this by no means encompasses all the different terms and definitions that are important to know.

Appreciation
The increase in the value of a property or a real estate portfolio due to changes in macro conditions such as economic growth, inflation, or numerous other causes is called appreciation. The opposite is depreciation.

Bidding War
A bidding war is a situation in which two or more potential buyers of a property or portfolio compete for that ownership through incrementally increasing bids.

Capitalization Rate (Cap Rate)

A cap rate, also known as the yield or yield on cost, is one the preeminent concepts used in commercial real estate. It is basically the return on a property based on the income that the property is generating. The cap rate of an investment can be calculated by dividing the property's net operating income by the current market value or acquisition cost of a property. Here is the formula:

Capitalization Rate = Annual Net Operating Income / Property Value

Let's use a simple example. Let's say that Jose wants to buy an apartment for $100,000 and expects that it will generate an annual net operating income of $9,000. The cap rate for this investment would be 9.0 percent ($9,000 / $100,000 = 9.0%).

Or let's say that Company X wants to buy an office building for $100 million that is generating an annual net operating income of $6 million. The cap rate for this investment would be 6.0 percent.

Central Business District (CBD)

A central business district is the commercial and business center of a city. Sometimes it is also known as the financial district.

Comparables (Comps)

Comparables are used to determine the value of an asset based on a recently sold similar asset. The idea is that recent sales of similar assets will likely reflect the current market for the asset and be a good indicator of the possible sale price for that specific asset. This technique is often used to determine the initial sale price of a property. It is one of several different ways to value a property.

Common Area Maintenance (CAM)

Common area maintenance is the cost that a landlord pays to operate and run its commercial property. CAM usually includes charges for cleaning up common areas, security, property taxes, insurance, repairs, and maintenance.

Commercial Mortgage-Backed Security (CMBS)

A CMBS refers to a type of mortgage-backed security that is backed by a commercial mortgage instead of by residential real estate.

CMBSs are complex securities and require a wide range of market participants. Among some of the entities involved with CMBS are servicers (primary, master and special), investors, rating agencies, and trustees. Each of these market participants has a different role to ensure that the CMBSs function properly.

Commercial Real Estate

Commercial real estate refers to property that is income producing. Commercial real estate includes office buildings, industrial and logistical centers, medical centers, hotels, shopping centers, retail stores, farm land, multifamily housing buildings, warehouses, and garages.

Construction Loan

A construction loan is short-term loan given to a company to finance the construction of a real estate project. The lender makes proceeds to the developer at periodic intervals as the work progresses. Because they are considered somewhat risky, construction loans usually have higher interest rates than traditional loans.

Closing

A closing refers to the meeting that takes place where the sale of a property or portfolio is finalized. At the closing meeting, buyers and sellers sign the final documents, and the buyer makes a payment and covers closing costs.

Depreciation

A decline in the value of property due to macro factors and other causes is called depreciation. The opposite is appreciation.

Discounted Cash Flow (DCF)

DCF analysis is widely used in real estate and is a method of valuing a project using the time value of money concept. It uses future free cash flow projections and discounts them, using an annual rate, to arrive at present value estimates. It is a useful analysis to determine how much to pay for a property (or portfolio) and it's also useful to determine whether a given project will be a good investment or not. Remember, however, that this analysis is only as good as the assumptions you use for projections.

Due Diligence

Due diligence refers to an investigation or audit of a potential property, portfolio, or company to confirm that the facts being reviewed are satisfactory to the group performing the inquiry. The goal of a due diligence in real estate is to ensure that all the fundamentals are in order, such as all legal documents, tax structures, any potential lease agreements, any obligations, market information, and more.

EBITDA

EBITDA—earnings before interest, tax, depreciation and amortization—is a measure of a company's operating performance. It is basically a way to evaluate a company's performance without having to account for any issues related to financing, accounting or tax.

Equity

Equity means ownership. The more equity you have, the more financial flexibility you have, as you can refinance against whatever equity you've built. Here is an example: if you recently acquired a $50 million building, and you owe $25 million to the bank, you have $25 million in equity.

Equity Multiple

An equity multiple is defined as the total cash distributions received from an investment, divided by the total equity invested. For example, if the total equity invested into a project was $1 million and all cash distributions received from the project totaled $1.6 million then the equity multiple would be $1.6 million / $1.0 million or 1.60x. Having an equity multiple at less than 1.0x means you are getting back less cash than you invested. An equity multiple greater than 1.0x means you are getting back more cash than you invested.

Fixed-Rate Mortgage

A type of loan in which the interest rate does not change during the entire term of the mortgage is called a fixed-rate mortgage.

Foreclosure

The legal process in which borrowers who have defaulted on their loans lose their ownership in the mortgaged property is called foreclosure. This process usually involves a forced sale of the property; and the proceeds of the sale are usually first taken by the lender so that they recoup their loan plus interest.

Flipping

Flipping refers to purchasing an asset with the intent of selling it for a quick profit rather than holding on to it for long-term appreciation. This term is usually associated with flipping homes.

Floor-to-Area Ratio (FAR)

The floor-to-area ratio is the relationship between the total amount of usable floor area that a building currently has, or is allowed to have, and the total area of the land parcel on which the building stands. This ratio is determined by dividing the total floor area of the building by the gross area of the land parcel. For example, a FAR of 10 for a property that has 1,000 square feet would mean that you could build 10,000 square feet of urban construction. Governments around the world use the floor-to-area ratio in zoning codes.

Funds from Operations (FFO)

Funds from operations refer to a calculation used by REITs (real estate investment trusts) to show cash flow from their operations. FFO is calculated by adding depreciation and amortization to earnings and then subtracting any gains on sales.

Ground Lease

A ground lease involves leasing land, typically from anywhere between 50 and 99 years, to a tenant who comes and constructs a building on the property. The ground lease defines who owns the land and who owns the building and improvements on the property.

Hard Costs

Costs associated with the physical construction of the building (and any fixed equipment in it) are called hard costs. They can be related to the building's structure, the landscape, labor and materials, and other building-related equipment. In terms of the building site, all utilities, equipment, HVAC systems, paving, and grading are considered hard costs. Those associated with the landscape are based on the architectural drawings and include grass, trees, mulch, fertilizer, and the like. The range of hard costs varies widely around the world but tends to be most expensive in global cities such as London, Hong Kong, Tokyo, San Francisco, New York, for instance.

HVAC
HVAC stands for the heating, ventilation, and air conditioning systems used to heat and cool buildings. HVAC systems have become the required industry standard for construction of new buildings.

Interest-Only (IO) Loan
With an IO loan the borrower only pays the interest on the mortgage through monthly payments for a term that is fixed, usually between 5 and 7 years. After the term is over, many borrowers look to refinance their assets, make a lump sum payment, or begin to pay off the principal of the loan.

Initial Public Offering (IPO)
An IPO is a type of public offering in which shares of a company are sold to institutional and retail investors in the public markets. An IPO is usually underwritten by at least one investment bank, which also arranges for the shares to be listed on one or more stock exchanges.

Internal Rate of Return (IRR)
The internal rate of return is a way of calculating rate of return by excluding external factors, such as cost of capital, inflation, and others. It is also called the discounted cash flow rate of return.

Liquidity

Liquidity in real estate describes the measure in which an asset can be quickly bought or sold in the market without affecting the asset's price. Cash is always considered to be the most liquid asset while real estate is generally considered illiquid.

Letter of Intent (LOI)

An LOI is a document outlining one or more agreements between two (or more) parties. The document is similar to a term sheet or memo of understanding. Such an agreement may be used for a leasing agreement, a joint venture partnership, an acquisition, as well as other purposes.

Lease

A lease is a legal contract that includes the terms of rental agreements in real estate. For example, a person who wishes to rent a house has to sign a lease that will describe the monthly rent, payment dates, the duration of the lease, and numerous other important terms. The landlord requires the tenant to sign the lease before inhabiting the property. While leases in the residential sector are usually one year, leases in the commercial space are longer—and more complex—usually between 3 and 10 years.

Loan-to-Cost (LTC)

The LTC is a percentage used in real estate construction to compare the amount of the loan used to finance a project to the cost of building the project. If the project costs $100 million to complete and the borrower borrows $60 million, then the loan-to-cost (LTC) ratio would be 60 percent. The costs included in the $100 million cost number would be the land parcel, construction labor and materials, as well as most of the soft costs.

Loan-to-Value (LTV)

An LTV is a percentage relationship between the amount of the loan and the appraised value or sales price (whichever is lower). For example, if you buy a house that costs $100,000 and you obtain 60 percent acquisition financing, your LTV would be 60 percent.

Lock-Up Period

A lock-up period is a window of time in which investors are not allowed to exchange or sell shares. In real estate, the lock-up period helps equity investors or lenders avoid liquidity problems while capital is put to work in investments that are considered less liquid.

Loan

A loan is a legal document that pledges a property to the lender as security for payment of a debt. Instead of mortgages, some states use First Trust Deeds.

Loss Factor

Loss factor is defined as the percentage difference between the rentable or the sellable area and the usable area. A building with a sellable area of 500,000 square feet and a usable area of 400,000 square feet, for example, has a loss factor of 20 percent.

Mezzanine Financing

Mezzanine financing is a hybrid form of lending sandwiched between the senior debt and equity, and it gives the lender the right to convert to an equity interest in the property in case of default after the senior lender is paid. It is the highest-risk form of debt; a typical interest rate for mezzanine financing is 12 to 20 percent, making it not only a high-risk but also a potentially high-return form of financing.

Example: Suppose a real estate investment firm wants to buy a building for $100 million. A senior lender only wants to lend 60 percent of the value of the building, $60 million. The fund doesn't want to put up all the remaining $40 million, so it finds a mezzanine investor willing to lend them $15 million. With $75 million in combined debt financing, the investment firm now only needs to contribute $25 million of its equity to purchase the building. This increases the buyer's potential return while minimizing the amount of capital it has to dedicate to the transaction; however, it also increases the risk the buyer is taking on to do the deal.

Net Operating Income (NOI)

Net operating income, also known as NOI, is a calculation used to analyze commercial real estate investments. NOI equals all revenue from the property minus all reasonably necessary operating expenses. NOI is a before-tax figure that excludes principal and interest payments on loans, capital expenditures, depreciation, and amortization.

For example, a property that has $100,000 in annual revenues and $27,000 in operating expenses, the NOI calculation is: $100,000—$27,000 = $73,000 NOI. Now let's break that down a little further.

Total Revenues	
Rental Income	$86,000
Parking Income	$10,000
Marketing Income	$2,000
Ancillary Income	$2,000
Total Income	$100,000
Operating Expenses	
Maintenance	$15,000
Management Fee	$4,000

Total Revenues	
Property Taxes	$3,000
Property Insurance	$3,000
Marketing	$2,000
Total Operating Exp.	$27,000
Net Operating Income	**$73,000**

Net Present Value (NPV)

Net present value is the value of all future cash flows (positive and negative) over the entire life of an investment discounted to the present. NPV analysis is a form of valuation used in real estate to measure the worth of a company, portfolio, or project.

Real Estate Agent

Real estate agents are licensed professionals who arrange—and many times help negotiate—the buying, selling, and leasing in real estate transactions. Agents usually work completely on commission, so their income depends on their ability to assist clients and close transactions.

Recourse Loan

A recourse loan allows a lender to seek damages if the borrower fails to pay back the mortgage and if the value of the underlying asset is not enough to cover it. A recourse loan allows the lender to go after all the assets that the borrower placed as collateral in case of default. It is not advisable for anyone to ever take a recourse loan.

REIT

A real estate investment trust (REIT) is a company that owns, and in most cases operates, income-producing real estate. REITs own many types of commercial real estate, ranging from commercial office and shopping centers to multifamily apartment buildings, warehouses, hotels, hospitals, and more. For a company to qualify as a REIT, it must meet certain regulatory guidelines. REITs often trade on major public stock exchanges and provide investors with a way to invest in real estate in a more liquid form.

Refinancing

Refinancing is the process of replacing an existing loan with a new one. It usually results in a borrower obtaining more favorable terms, primarily a lower interest rate or a renegotiated number of years to repay the loan, from the lender. Borrowers, by refinancing, can cash out and recover some of the original investment in the asset or portfolio they acquired.

Replacement Cost

The cost to replace a real estate asset includes all land costs, hard costs, and soft costs.

Soft Costs

Soft costs include architectural and engineering fees, legal and fiscal fees, permits and license costs, development fees, building maintenance, insurance, security, and other fees associated with the asset's upkeep. In any ground-up development there are land and hard costs as well as soft costs.

Sweat Equity

Sweat equity refers to any contribution to the development or repositioning of a property in the form of labor or services, rather than cash. The person who contributes this labor will get equity in the deal in exchange.

Title Insurance

Title insurance protects the buyer (via the owner's policy) or the lender (via the lender's policy) against loss arising from disputes over ownership of a property.

Triple Net Lease

A triple net lease is a lease agreement that labels the tenant as the responsible party for covering all the costs relating to the leasing of the asset. Therefore, in addition to paying rent, the lease also requires the tenant to pay the net amount of common area maintenance, real estate taxes, and building insurance.

A Recap of the 7 Key Lessons

1. Have a Powerful Mindset
   "When it comes to the balance between mindset and technical skills, I believe that your mindset is far more important."

   Rohit Ravi

2. Be the Hardest Worker in Any Room
   "There is no success without very hard work."

   Gina Diez Barroso

3. Develop Deep Focus and Clarity
   "Have a clear focus and strategy, and you will experience great success."

   Robert Faith

4. Be Educated and Quantitative
   "Understanding the numbers in real estate is absolutely critical."

   Ronald Terwilliger

5. Surround Yourself with Greatness

   "Be humble and allow people around you to speak up and give you the input you need."

   Richard Mack

6. Be an Extraordinary Salesperson

   "Become a person who you would want to do business with, the fruits will follow."

   Joseph Sitt

7. Execute their Ideas

   "One of the big secrets in real estate is to get started and execute."

   Urs Ledermann

About the Author

Erez Cohen is co-founder and co-CEO of a real estate investment management and development firm. Erez has been directly involved in the acquisition and development of more than 12 million square feet of real estate, with a value of over $3.5 billion. Erez has worked in investment positions at Thor Urbana, Apollo Real Estate Advisors, the Carlyle Group, and Evercore Partners. With over 13 years in real estate, he has been involved in public and private deals in the residential, retail, office, hotel, and mixed-use sectors. In addition, Erez is an advisor to startups and mentor to myriad entrepreneurs and real estate professionals.

Erez currently sits on the board of the Urban Land Institute as well as two nonprofit organizations. He holds a BA from Manhattan College, where he graduated summa cum laude, and an MBA from Wharton Business School at the University of Pennsylvania.

Throughout his career Erez has been honored with several recognitions, among them, the Rising Star Award from the Urban Land Institute and the Bucksbaum Memorial Fellowship from the Wharton School.

Connect with Erez on social media:

- Facebook: theErezCohen
- LinkedIn: Erez Cohen
- Twitter: theErezCohen
- Instagram: theErezCohen
- YouTube: ErezCohen
- Facebook Group: Facebook.com/groups/RealEstateTitans

Index